First World War
and Army of Occupation
War Diary
France, Belgium and Germany

33 DIVISION
98 Infantry Brigade
Suffolk Regiment
4th Battalion
1 November 1915 - 30 January 1918

WO95/2427/2

The Naval & Military Press Ltd
www.nmarchive.com
Published in association with The National Archives

Published by

The Naval & Military Press Ltd

Unit 10 Ridgewood Industrial Park,

Uckfield, East Sussex,

TN22 5QE England

Tel: +44 (0) 1825 749494

www.naval-military-press.com

www.nmarchive.com

This diary has been reprinted in facsimile from the original. Any imperfections are inevitably reproduced and the quality may fall short of modern type and cartographic standards.

© Crown Copyright
Images reproduced by permission of The National Archives, London, England, 2015.

Contents

Document type	Place/Title	Date From	Date To
Heading	WO95/2427-2 4 Bn Suffolk Regt 1915 Nov-1919 Jan		
Heading	33rd Division 98th Infy Bde 1-4th Bn Suffolk Regt 1915 Nov-Jan-1918 From Lahore Div To 58 Div (Pioneers)		
Heading	46/15th 1/4th Suffolk Rgt Nov Dec 31 III IV 15th Nov transferred to 46 Bde 15 Div		
War Diary		01/11/1915	30/11/1915
War Diary		01/12/1915	31/12/1915
War Diary		01/01/1916	31/01/1916
War Diary		01/02/1916	29/02/1916
Heading	33 G.H.Q. 46 Div Suffolk Regt Vol IV & V transferred to XXXIII Feb 27		
Heading	98th Brigade 33rd Division. Came from 46th Brigade 15th Division 27.2.16		
War Diary		01/03/1916	16/03/1916
War Diary	Bethune	17/03/1916	17/03/1916
War Diary	Annequin North	17/03/1916	18/03/1916
War Diary	Trenches.	22/03/1916	29/03/1916
War Diary	Bethune	30/03/1916	31/03/1916
Heading	98th Brigade. 33rd Division. 1/4th Battalion The Suffolk Regiment April 1916		
War Diary	Bethune	01/04/1916	02/04/1916
War Diary	Annezin	03/04/1916	10/04/1916
War Diary	Bethune	11/04/1916	14/04/1916
War Diary	Annequin. S.	14/04/1916	16/04/1916
War Diary	In The Trenches.	17/04/1916	20/04/1916
War Diary	Annequin S.	21/04/1916	22/04/1916
War Diary	In The Trenches.	23/04/1916	26/04/1916
War Diary	Annezin	27/04/1916	01/05/1916
Heading	98th Brigade. 33rd Division. 1/4th Battalion The Suffolk Regiment May 1916 Reports on Raid 13/14th Attached.		
War Diary		01/05/1916	01/05/1916
War Diary	Annezin	02/05/1916	04/05/1916
War Diary	In The Trenches	05/05/1916	08/05/1916
War Diary	Annequin. N.	09/05/1916	12/05/1916
War Diary	In The Trenches.	13/05/1916	16/05/1916
War Diary	Annequin N.	17/05/1916	19/05/1916
War Diary	Annequin North	20/05/1916	20/05/1916
War Diary	In The Trenches	21/05/1916	24/05/1916
War Diary	Annequin North	25/05/1916	28/05/1916
War Diary	Bethune	29/05/1916	02/06/1916
Miscellaneous	Capture of crater by 1/4th Suffolk Regiment.	15/05/1916	15/05/1916
Miscellaneous	Raid by the 1/4th Suffolk Regt., on the night of 13/14th May, 1916	17/05/1916	17/05/1916
Heading	98th Brigade. 33rd Division. 1/4th Battalion The Suffolk Regiment June 1916		
Heading	Entries for June 1st & 2nd will be found in War Diary for May 1916		
War Diary	Bethune	02/06/1916	10/06/1916

War Diary	Annequin North		11/06/1916	17/06/1916
War Diary	In The Trenches		18/06/1916	18/06/1916
War Diary	Givenchy Sector		18/06/1916	18/06/1916
War Diary	Left. Sub. Section		18/06/1916	19/06/1916
War Diary	In The Trenches		19/06/1916	21/06/1916
War Diary	Gorre		22/06/1916	30/06/1916
Heading	98th Inf. Bde. 33rd Div. War Diary. 1/4th Battn. The Suffolk Regiment. July 1916			
War Diary			01/07/1916	02/07/1916
War Diary	In The Trenches. Quinchy. Left Sub. Section.		03/07/1916	31/07/1916
Heading	Appendix "A"			
Miscellaneous	1/4th Bn. Suffolk Regt. Appendix "a"			
Heading	98th Brigade. 33rd Division. 1/4th Battalion Suffolk Regiment August 1916			
War Diary	Dernancourt		01/08/1916	07/08/1916
War Diary	Fricourt.		08/08/1916	31/08/1916
Heading	1/4th Bn. Suffolk Regt.			
Heading	98th Brigade. 33rd Division. 1/4th Battalion The Suffolk Regiment September 1916			
Miscellaneous	1/4th Bn. Suffolk Regt. Casualties for September 1916			
War Diary			25/09/1916	30/09/1916
War Diary			01/09/1916	24/09/1916
Heading	98th Brigade. 33rd Division. 1/4th Battalion The Suffolk Regiment October 1916			
War Diary			01/10/1916	15/10/1916
War Diary	Sus-St. Leger.		16/10/1916	31/10/1916
Heading	98th Brigade. 33rd Division. 1/4th Battalion The Suffolk Regiment November 1916			
War Diary			01/11/1916	30/11/1916
Heading	98th Brigade. 33rd Division. 1/4th Battalion The Suffolk Regiment December 1916			
War Diary	Huchenneville		01/12/1916	05/12/1916
War Diary	Bray. Sur. Somme		06/12/1916	08/12/1916
War Diary	Maricourt		08/12/1916	08/12/1916
War Diary	Maurepas		09/12/1916	10/12/1916
War Diary	Trenches		10/12/1916	11/12/1916
War Diary	Le Forest		12/12/1916	14/12/1916
War Diary	Trenches		14/12/1916	18/12/1916
War Diary	Suzanne		18/12/1916	21/12/1916
War Diary	Maurepas		22/12/1916	25/12/1916
War Diary	Trenches		25/12/1916	27/12/1916
War Diary	Bray-Sur-Somme		27/12/1916	29/12/1916
War Diary	Villers-Sous-Ailly		29/12/1916	19/01/1917
War Diary	Camp 12		20/01/1917	20/01/1917
War Diary	Camp 18		21/01/1917	21/01/1917
War Diary	Howitzer Wood		22/01/1917	23/01/1917
War Diary	Trenches		24/01/1917	28/01/1917
War Diary	Camp 19		29/01/1917	31/01/1917
War Diary	Trenches.		01/02/1917	16/02/1917
War Diary	Camp 19		17/02/1917	25/02/1917
War Diary	Howitzer Wood		26/02/1917	26/02/1917
War Diary	Trenches		27/02/1917	28/02/1917
Miscellaneous	Report on Raid Carried Out By The 1/4th Suffolk Regiment At 9.30 P.M., February 13th, 1917		14/02/1917	14/02/1917
War Diary	Road Wood		01/03/1917	02/03/1917
War Diary	Trenches		03/03/1917	04/03/1917

War Diary	Howitzer Wood.	05/03/1917	05/03/1917
War Diary	Suzanne	06/03/1917	06/03/1917
War Diary	Suzanne and Sailly Laurette	07/03/1917	07/03/1917
War Diary	Sailly Laurette	08/03/1917	11/03/1917
War Diary	Camp 124	12/03/1917	01/04/1917
War Diary	La Neuville	02/04/1917	02/04/1917
War Diary	Molliens-au-Bois	03/04/1917	03/04/1917
War Diary	Naours	04/04/1917	04/04/1917
War Diary	Longuevillette	05/04/1917	05/04/1917
War Diary	Beaurepaire	06/04/1917	07/04/1917
War Diary	Couin	08/04/1917	08/04/1917
War Diary	Berles-au-Bois.	09/04/1917	11/04/1917
War Diary	Madelain Redoubt	12/04/1917	12/04/1917
War Diary	N.26.C.O.9	13/04/1917	16/04/1917
War Diary	Trenches	17/04/1917	20/04/1917
War Diary	N.26	21/04/1917	22/04/1917
War Diary	Trenches	23/04/1917	24/04/1917
War Diary	Boyelles Bivouac	25/04/1917	25/04/1917
War Diary	Bretencourt	26/04/1917	02/05/1917
War Diary	Douchy	03/05/1917	10/05/1917
War Diary	Boyelles	11/05/1917	15/05/1917
War Diary	Trenches	16/05/1917	25/05/1917
War Diary	Boyelles	26/05/1917	28/05/1917
War Diary	Trenches	29/05/1917	31/05/1917
War Diary	Hendecourt	01/06/1917	20/06/1917
War Diary	Boyelles	21/06/1917	24/06/1917
War Diary	Trenches	25/06/1917	30/06/1917
War Diary	Basseux	01/07/1917	03/07/1917
War Diary	Acheux	04/07/1917	04/07/1917
War Diary	Talmas	05/07/1917	05/07/1917
War Diary	La Chaussee	06/07/1917	06/07/1917
War Diary	Warlus	07/07/1917	31/07/1917
War Diary	La Panne	01/08/1917	16/08/1917
War Diary	Coxyde	17/08/1917	17/08/1917
War Diary	Wellington Camp	18/08/1917	20/08/1917
War Diary	Queensland Camp	21/08/1917	23/08/1917
War Diary	Trenches	24/08/1917	29/08/1917
War Diary	Bray Dunes	30/08/1917	31/08/1917
War Diary	Bray Dunes	01/09/1917	01/09/1917
War Diary	Zudrove	02/09/1917	15/09/1917
War Diary	Oehtezeele	16/09/1917	16/09/1917
War Diary	Steenvoorde	17/09/1917	17/09/1917
War Diary	Meteren	18/09/1917	20/09/1917
War Diary	Reninghelst Camp.	21/09/1917	22/09/1917
War Diary	Bellegoed Farm	23/09/1917	23/09/1917
War Diary	Trenches	24/09/1917	27/09/1917
War Diary	Bellgoed Farm	28/09/1917	28/09/1917
War Diary	Lynde	29/09/1917	30/09/1917
Miscellaneous	Movements of The 1/4th Suffolk Regiment From 24th To 28th September, 1917	24/09/1917	24/09/1917
War Diary	Lynde	01/10/1917	06/10/1917
War Diary	Railway Dugouts	07/10/1917	15/10/1917
War Diary	Kortepyp Camp	16/10/1917	20/10/1917
War Diary	Kortepyp Camp B.	20/10/1917	30/10/1917
War Diary	Shankhill Huts Neuve Eglise.	31/10/1917	02/11/1917
War Diary	Ypres	03/11/1917	06/11/1917

War Diary	Neuve Eglise.	07/11/1917	11/11/1917
War Diary	Merris Area	12/11/1917	15/11/1917
War Diary	Potijze	16/11/1917	16/11/1917
War Diary	Trenches	17/11/1917	22/11/1917
War Diary	Potijze	23/11/1917	23/11/1917
War Diary	Toronto Camp	24/11/1917	29/11/1917
War Diary	Potijze	30/11/1917	30/11/1917
War Diary	Potizje St Jean Camp	01/12/1917	05/12/1917
War Diary	In The Line Paschendaele	06/12/1917	11/12/1917
War Diary	Potizje	12/12/1917	12/12/1917
War Diary	Eecke	13/12/1917	05/01/1918
War Diary	Toronto Camp	06/01/1918	10/01/1918
War Diary	Whitby Camp	11/01/1918	12/01/1918
War Diary	Hamburg Support Line	13/01/1918	13/01/1918
War Diary	Trenches	14/01/1918	17/01/1918
War Diary	Alnwick Camp	18/01/1918	19/01/1918
War Diary	Toronto Camp.	20/01/1918	21/01/1918
War Diary	Alnwick Camp	22/01/1918	23/01/1918
War Diary	Hamburg Support	24/01/1918	28/01/1918
War Diary	St Lawrence Camp	29/01/1918	30/01/1918

WO 95 2427/2

4 BN. SUFFOLK REGT

1915 NOV - 1919 JAN

33RD DIVISION
98TH INFY BDE

1-4TH BN SUFFOLK REGT
1915 Nov.
~~MAR 1916~~ - JAN - 1918

from LAHORE DIV

To 58 DIV (PIONEERS)

1/4th Suffolk Regt.

Oct, Nov, Dec 31

III. IV. Vol XIII

Bareilly.
15th Nov. transferred to 46th Bde.
15th Div.

WAR DIARY
or
INTELLIGENCE SUMMARY.
(Erase heading not required.)

Army Form C. 2118.

Instructions regarding War Diaries and Intelligence Summaries are contained in F.S. Regs., Part II and the Staff Manual respectively. Title pages will be prepared in manuscript.

Hour, Date, Place	Summary of Events and Information	Remarks and references to Appendices
Nov 1st 9.2 am	Battalion in trenches between OXFORD ST. (communication trench) and LIVERPOOL ST. Weather very bad. Much rain. Parapet collapses in places. Also dug-outs.	
3rd	About 2.4 p.m. the enemy was observed in the open about 6 a.m. Our snipers promptly got to work responsible for 9 of them. No retaliation enemy shells on front line for a short period only. Light rifle grenade fire - no damage resulted throughout. Battalion brought back to CROIX BARBEE in Bde. Reserve A SIRMUND Cdr. of the Bn. Relieved by the 1st GURKHAS.	
4th	Still in Bde. Reserve.	
5/6/16 9 A	Battalion in huts of 137th Bde. moved to front line & held line	
10th	Between SUNKEN RD & NEW CUT ALLEY. Trenches in very bad condition. Two reserve coys in much rain.	
11th	MOGGS HOLE. Busy clearing out communication trenches. Weather still bad. Parapets fell in every spot except for a few hours about 6 p.m. Trench mortar silenced by our Artillery. 3rd Gurkhas relieved 2nd day	
12th		Battalion relieved by Guards Bgd. N.STAFFS
13th	Battalion came out of trenches & proceeded to CROIX BARBEE	
14th	Battalion entrained and marched from CROIX BARBEE to ESSE	
15th	from which place busses took them to VERQUIN to join with Batt. Bde at La Barme	
16th	Day spent in cleaning up	
17 to 22nd	Company training, practice in Grenade throwing &c.	

(73989) W4141—463. 400,000. 9/14. H.&J.Ltd. Forms/C. 2118/10.

Army Form C. 2118.

WAR DIARY
or
INTELLIGENCE SUMMARY.
(Erase heading not required.)

Instructions regarding War Diaries and Intelligence Summaries are contained in F. S. Regs., Part II. and the Staff Manual respectively. Title pages will be prepared in manuscript.

Hour, Date, Place	Summary of Events and Information	Remarks and references to Appendices
23rd	Battalion moved to trenches at D Sector D 3	
24th	Weather very cold. Enemy's trench undertaking. Our position exactly opposite. Most post Hohenzollern Redoubt. Distance of enemy at nearest point 50 yards.	
25th	Battalion brought back to Reserve trenches (LANCASHIRE TRENCH) close to VERMELLES.	
26th	Battalion in same position. Working parties supplied to R.E.	
27th	Battalion moved back to front line D.3.	
28th	Enemy active with Artillery & Trench Mortars. Our Artillery replied brilliantly them. Several parties dealt with.	
29th	Battalion moved back to LANCASHIRE TRENCH	
30th	Battalion in same position. Working parties supplied to R.E.	

WAR DIARY or INTELLIGENCE SUMMARY

Army Form C. 2118.

Hour, Date, Place	Summary of Events and Information	Remarks and references to Appendices
See lab.		
2nd 9 g.m	Battalion moved up to front line at D1 Trenches extremely bad. Prospect + parapet falling in. A great deal of work required to keep them in repair	
4°	No rain. A good deal of wastefulness caused by Germans standing on their parapet shooting up their hands as except one, don't by them. If the Regiment on our left suggested that the British would fire upon comrades as prisoners than as soldiers. Our Artillery & Snipers promptly replied with "rapid" trench shooting for an hour. Situation gradually became normal	
5°	Battalion moved back to Reserve in LANCASHIRE TRENCH	
6°	Situation normal	
7°	Battalion relieved by 8th K.O.S.B. & marched to GOSNAY	
8° & 9°	Day spent in cleaning up	
10°	Company training — Leave sanctioned for 20 all ranks per diem. For large working parties supplied for the purpose of cleaning up trenches near front line. Men killed in Steens & wounded in front party.	
11° & 12°	Company training	

Army Form C. 2118.

WAR DIARY
or
INTELLIGENCE SUMMARY.
(Erase heading not required.)

Instructions regarding War Diaries and Intelligence Summaries are contained in F.S. Regs., Part II. and the Staff Manual respectively. Title pages will be prepared in manuscript.

Hour, Date, Place	Summary of Events and Information	Remarks and references to Appendices
Dec. 13th	Battalion marched to RAIMBERT in which place they form part of Corps Reserve	
" 14th to 18th	Company training, men — Officers sent for courses in Officers Training School, Grenadiers' Novices' course, Signallers' advanced course, French Mortar School & Machine Gun courses. Inspection of Machine Gunners, these were passed as fit for service.	
19th	Battalion lined road at RAIMBERT in honor of G.M. SIR J. FRENCH, who passed through	
20–21st	Coy training. Lists of men available who had been in FRANCE since 4th NOV 9th 1914 without leave were prepared to everyone a period of furlough.	

Dec 21st/1915
In the field

M Candisto H/Col
O.C. 4th Suffolks

(73989) W4141—463. 400,000. 9/14. H.&J.Ltd. Forms/C. 2118/10.

Army Form C. 2118.

WAR DIARY
or
INTELLIGENCE SUMMARY.
(Erase heading not required.)

Instructions regarding War Diaries and Intelligence Summaries are contained in F.S. Regs., Part II. and the Staff Manual respectively. Title pages will be prepared in manuscript.

Hour, Date, Place	Summary of Events and Information	Remarks and references to Appendices
Dec 2nd 1916	Battalion testing at RAIMBERT. The Battalion carried on course of training in the following studies:- Physical Exercise, Company drill, Battalion drill, Jumping distances, Route Marches, Brigade Route marches, Musketry, Musketry on the Range Running, Bayonet fighting. Lectures by C.O. to all Officers. Advanced & Brigade Courses for Officers sent to Machine Guns, Signalling, Trench Mortars, Grenades, Offices Training School, Gas, Lewis Guns.	

(73989) W4141—463. 400,000. 9/14. H.&J.Ltd. Forms/C. 2118/10.

H. Suffolks Jan & Feb '16

WAR DIARY
or
INTELLIGENCE SUMMARY.

Army Form C. 2118.

(Erase heading not required.)

Hour, Date, Place	Summary of Events and Information	Remarks and references to Appendices
Jan. 1st – 5th	Battalion at RAINBERT. Battalion Races in Plymouth Stadium Company Mile Battalion Race. Jumping distances. Foot Races. Musketry. Shooting on the Range. Physical Training, Running Exercises. Bayonet fighting. Lectures by C.O. to all officers. Personnel of Brigade. Classes for Officers. Others in machine gun. Signalling. French. Instruction Officers Trenches School.	
Jan. 6th	General Trevise. Battalion marched from RAINBERT to billets. 0.50 a.m. in company with Brigade from order of Brigade marched to exception of 10 minutes halt every hour Battalion arrived at 2.30 p.m. when orders were received to billet in the village of SERNEY. Posts were put out to guard the approaches of all the main roads to the village & harassing men carried on. At 8 p.m. in a state of 15 minutes readiness was relieved. At 10.30 p.m. state of readiness was called off. No men were made at 0.30 p.m. Battalion effect at rest. Division 2nd was made until 12.30 p.m. Two Battalions were billeted upon our be fed & refresh but tanomisita to Division about 6 which the order were now one then per Iron Battalion received instruction to billet at SERNEY. The roads were again guarded until 7 p.m. when all pickets were called in.	

Army Form C. 2118.

WAR DIARY
or
INTELLIGENCE SUMMARY.
(Erase heading not required.)

Instructions regarding War Diaries and Intelligence Summaries are contained in F.S. Regs., Part II and the Staff Manual respectively. Title pages will be prepared in manuscript.

Hour, Date, Place	Summary of Events and Information	Remarks and references to Appendices
Jan 7th	At 9 a.m. the return journey was commenced. Weather very bad, cold intense through rain. Battalion eventually arrived at RAMBERT 2.30 p.m.	
Jan 7th to 12th	Training continued on the same lines as from Jan 1st to 7th.	
Jan. 13th	Division moved up to front line. Battalion left RAMBERT 6.30 a.m., marched to LILLERS, entrained to MAZINGARBE, PHILOSOPHE, VERMELLES where the LONDON SCOTTISH was relieved & the Bns. lying between DEVON LANE and KINGSWAY, while the Bn. marched through MAZINGARBE, PHILOSOPHE, VERMELLES.	LONDON SCOTTISH was relieved
14th	Enemy very active again. Bn. with Rifle Grenades, Trench Bombs & Aerial Torpedoes. He retaliated with artillery.	
15th	2 French Machine Bombs. A T.C. boys in West end of section. Enemy all seemed quieter. Sent work &	
16th	Had went unmolested, principally enemies. Sent word to Bn. Shops until opened fired. Enemy tried to fire, and 2 Trades shots did some damage to French P.O. on communications. Battalion occupied billets. Worked hard in Devon trenches.	
17th	2nd M.C.S.R. relieved by Battalion in front line. Enemy still active. Accidentally killed Hen by others. No details yet recd.	
18th	A Main trench line lost every appearance of. Front was ill dawn in emptying trenches. Enemy put out before dark small arms	

BRECON Y MERTHYR Supr., B/Roads (?) Forms/C. 2118/10.

WAR DIARY
or
INTELLIGENCE SUMMARY.
(Erase heading not required.)

Army Form C. 2118.

Hour, Date, Place	Summary of Events and Information	Remarks and references to Appendices
Jan. 19th	At 6.30 a.m enemy exploded a mine on our front line between NEWPORT & BRECON saps. This was missed by R.E. O.C. that Coy R.E. mines was met burried in crater shaft. Front immediately blocked for space of 50 yards. Party at our post on 8 dig through enemy at first very active on Parapet, but was kiled but quickly subdued by our Artillery. On myth rt. lip of the crater was manned by bombers. O.pen tench through a cross and forming NAT but no damage done. Size of crater about 17 yards by 12. 7-10 feet deep.	
" 20th	Enemy noticeably quiet. At 3 p.m. Lt Col CROUDAS went out to view Craters & was shot in the stomach. He was later to F.W. Ambulance with the utmost dispatch but died about 6 a.m. Battalion relieved by 6th CAMERONS at 6 p.m. Proceeded to NOEUX les MINES.	
" 21st	Buried CROUDAS. Burial at NOEUX les MINES in presence of Battalion & all officers in 10 Brigade. CAPT E.P.CLARKE assumed command.	
" 22nd & 23rd	Position book. Great attention paid to Gas Helmet drill and grenade throwing.	

WAR DIARY
or
INTELLIGENCE SUMMARY.
(Erase heading not required.)

Army Form C. 2118.

Hour, Date, Place	Summary of Events and Information	Remarks and references to Appendices
Jan 26th	Batt proceeded to Reserve Bivouacs at 10th AVENUE. D Coy & 6th CONNAUGHT RANGERS attached to Battalion inclusion to each Coy.	
27th	Enemy attacked 10th SCOTTISH RIFLES town repulsed. Butts moved up to General Reserve Trench - many men sent to S.R. Bn to act as Guides to runs and carry parties, purmital to help with repair/guart time working till 5 am.	
28th	Large working parties improving the SUPPORT LINE by night	
29th	Quiet day - no working parties.	
30th	Moved up to LOOS - Bn at action A.C.B. Group in front line. D Coy in Reserve. & support in cellars by day. & support trench by night	
31st	Much work wiring, general improvement of trenches - intermittent shelling of LOOS in vicinity of H.Q by heavy shells	

WAR DIARY
or
INTELLIGENCE SUMMARY.
(Erase heading not required.)

Army Form C. 2118.

Hour, Date, Place	Summary of Events and Information	Remarks and references to Appendices
Oct 1st	D Coy relieved B Coy in front line on night previous. Enemy put over some Rifle grenades - otherwise quiet up until 5 P.M.	
2	Enemy shelled us for an hour with 6 in shells & for considerably longer in neighbourhood of B Coy in the village.	
3rd	Enemy commenced shelling village & HQrs about and our trenches about 10 am this was continued throughout the day until about 3.30 PM the shelling became intense - as many as 40 to 50 heavy shells were counted to the minute - communication trenches being quite impassable. LIEUT K W TURNER showed great gallantry in getting his B Coy up in SUPPORT LINE from villages in the village with our horses through a tremendous hail of shells - C. O. RPL A.V.I.S. D. Coy no Pl turn up without relief two recommended for R.C.M. for acting promptly in his own initiative in difficult situation	

WAR DIARY
or
INTELLIGENCE SUMMARY.
(Erase heading not required.)

Army Form C. 2118.

Hour, Date, Place	Summary of Events and Information	Remarks and references to Appendices
Oct 31st	About 5.15 pm all communication with front trenches by telephone was lost & the shelling becoming heavier B D E H Q were asked to request artillery to provide a Barrage, message to that time – this was done – enemy battle front line & the enemy must have sustained many casualties. Capt. a [Griblin?] (6 munster) Reserve attached to B not 7&9 were recommended [illegible] 9.6 m [illegible] an explanation in return a message to front line. During the bombardment the enemy would avail [illegible] maintaining shells which [illegible] a wonderful spectacle. The B [?] were expecting to be relieved by 6th K O S B turning to the uncertainty of the situation the latter did not arrive till about 2 am – the relief was finally completed at 5 am – the B not returned to Reshen line at 10 am were at 7 am. All ranks behaved with the greatest gallantry during this trying [?]	

WAR DIARY
or
INTELLIGENCE SUMMARY.
(Erase heading not required.)

Army Form C. 2118.

Hour, Date, Place	Summary of Events and Information	Remarks and references to Appendices
Feb 3rd (cont)	He was wounded 15 - The small number of Hun material was due to the fact that all except a very few sentries were pulled into the deep dug outs immediately during the Bombardment. Relief by 8th KOSB completed about 5 am.	5-25 am
Feb 4th	Working parties at night.	
5th	Working parties - 214 other ranks with 2/LIEUTS MATTINGLY and BOND arrived as a white were handed amongst Coys. in Reserve line.	
6th	Working parts in support Reserve line.	
7th	Batt relieved by 3 Coys of 44th BDE in each 13th R.SCOTS, 6 CAMERONS and 8th B. WATCH (2). and returned to billets at NOEUX LES MINES.	
8th - 13th	Inspection - general training and Routine work including special attention to GAS HELMETS.	

WAR DIARY
or
INTELLIGENCE SUMMARY.

(Erase heading not required.)

Army Form C. 2118.

Instructions regarding War Diaries and Intelligence Summaries are contained in F. S. Regs., Part II and the Staff Manual respectively. Title pages will be prepared in manuscript.

Hour, Date, Place	Summary of Events and Information	Remarks and references to Appendices
6.10 am - 11th	MAJOR A C TAYLOR SUFFOLK REGT returned from 15th DIV SCHOOL + assumed command of Battalion on 11th inst	
13th	Personal ZZZ. Bn. in circular in line trenches handed to Front system - B + D Coys under MAJOR TAYLOR in trenches - (B in fire line D in SUPPORT + Reserve between VENDIN ALLEY and HULLY LANE. A + C Coys under CAPT E P CLARKE in BDE Reserve in PHILOSOPHE.	
14th - 15th	B + D Coys general improvement of trenches including wiring. A + C Coys large working parties.	
16th	76th BATT'Ns changed over C in front line A n SUPPORT + Reserve	
17th - 18th	Enemy using rifle grenades - ours were exceptionally successful to, practically during enemy to cease. - much work in dugout LINE and ESSEX LANE E - 185. 2/LIEUT PATTEN wounded unable to rejoin	

WAR DIARY or INTELLIGENCE SUMMARY

Army Form C. 2118.

Hour, Date, Place	Summary of Events and Information	Remarks and references to Appendices
Dec 19th	C Coy carried out a successful "STRAAFE" on enemy's sap opposite SAP 45. 2 LT WOODS threw 9 live bombs from end of our sap, covering party threw others from behind him. LT HUME carried out rifle grenade to field from covering front - supported by W Ln and M GUNS - men to try to get to enter SAP but returned immediately. Suggestions in returning suggests our enemy when enthin bail moan. Our enemy very annoying. A flat 7 on attempt pursued our trenches about 9 p.m. - several lights being sent up.	
20th	2B were changed over D Coy went into B in support & Reserve.	
21st	Quiet day. Good progress made with raising front line.	

WAR DIARY
or
INTELLIGENCE SUMMARY.
(Erase heading not required.)

Army Form C. 2118.

Hour, Date, Place	Summary of Events and Information	Remarks and references to Appendices
Feb 22nd	Very severe weather with snow & frost. Work continued in trenches - wiring, patrols. 4th BATT in PHILOSOPHE	
23rd	1/2 Batts changed over. A Coy in front with C in support + Reserve.	
24th	Work continued as before	
25th	Batt relieved by Scots Fusiliers in front line and 13th R Scots in Reserve. and marched to MAZINGARBE	
26th	Baths for all ranks	
27th	Batt transferred from 15th DIV to 33rd DIV. Inspection by MAJOR GENL McCRACKEN in CHURCH SQ NOEUX LES MINES - a written memo was handed the CO by BRIG GENL MATHESON commanding 4th BDE conveying the agreement as regards conduct, especially maintaining the standard of close contact w/ entrenchment of 1005 on FEB 3rd	

WAR DIARY
or
INTELLIGENCE SUMMARY.

(Erase heading not required.)

Army Form C. 2118.

Hour, Date, Place	Summary of Events and Information	Remarks and references to Appendices
Feb 27th cont	Batt. then moved to BETHUNE & were billetted until return of 33rd DIV.	
28th.	Batt. moved into BDE RESERVE at ANNEQUIN SOUTH relieving 4th KINGS REGT. prior to 98th BDE	
29th.	Batt. moved to front line at Z.1. A B D Coys in front support line - C Coy in KEEPS.	

46 D V   3 3 / GHQ

4 Suffolk Regt

Vol IV & V

Transferred to XXXIII

Feb 27°

46

98th Brigade.

33rd Division.

Came from 46th Brigade 15th Division 27.2.16.

1/4th BATTALION

THE SUFFOLK REGIMENT

MARCH 1 9 1 6

WAR DIARY
or
INTELLIGENCE SUMMARY.

(Erase heading not required.)

Army Form C. 2118.

4 Suffolks

98
33

Hour, Date, Place	Summary of Events and Information	Remarks and references to Appendices
March 1st – 8th	Very quiet time – work continued in wiring and general improvements. Drainage very bad – conditions owing to the heavy snow.	
8th	Batt relieved by 16th K.R.R. and went to billets in BETHUNE	
9th, 10th	Cleaning up from maneuvers – working parties furnished daily.	
11th	Batt inspected by G.O.C. 98th BDE i. Brig Genl E.P. STRICKLAND CMG DSO weather since the Batt had arrived in the JULLUNDER BDE.	
12th	Church Parade at O Pera House.	
13th	Major Genl LANDEN CB. 33rd Div inspected area of action of Bn with a view of its defences again. Writing parties furnished. Regimental employed of burials owing to being a nasty full cases of Cerebro MENINGITIS	LIEUT FRERE.

Army Form C. 2118.

WAR DIARY
or
INTELLIGENCE SUMMARY.
(Erase heading not required.)

Instructions regarding War Diaries and Intelligence Summaries are contained in F. S. Regs., Part II. and the Staff Manual respectively. Title pages will be prepared in manuscript.

Hour, Date, Place	Summary of Events and Information	Remarks and references to Appendices
March 14.	WAR carried on in billets - wrote much. All available grenade throwing instructed with live grenades. Butt retired from Chocolate. Lecture by Ch. Chaplain on his experience as prisoner in Germany.	
15th.	Reports to Coy Commanders by C O. On certain assumption Germans	
15th.	Range at ANNEZIN allotted to Butt'n	
16th.	Lecture to all ranks by Pmty? 1st MIDDLESEX REGT on experience with flammenwerfer. - Lorry motor Tms.	
BETHUNE 17th	Batt. paraded at 4.30 & marched via BOUVRAY to ANNEQUIN NORTH. Steel shaped helmets have been issued to all officers & most of the men, this is the first time they were worn on parade by all	

(73989) W4141—463. 400,000. 9/14. H.&J.Ltd. Forms/C. 2118/10.

Army Form C. 2118.

WAR DIARY
or
INTELLIGENCE SUMMARY.
(Erase heading not required.)

Instructions regarding War Diaries and Intelligence Summaries are contained in F.S. Regs., Part II. and the Staff Manual respectively. Title pages will be prepared in manuscript.

Hour, Date, Place	Summary of Events and Information	Remarks and references to Appendices
ANNEQUIN NORTH 17-Road	Regt arrived at 6.30 pm & took over billets from 1/MIDDLESEX REGT. (COL.ROWLEY). The Regt was in reserve before the attack on GIVENCHY in Dec 1914 at this place.	
18th	Maj. TURNER arrived from ENGLAND & taken over command of the Battalion. CAMBRIN was heavily shelled by the enemy during the evening & a few lachrymator shells fell on the La Bassee road, known to which we felt the effect.	
TRENCHES. 22nd	The regt relieves the 1/Middlesex Regt in the CUINCHY SECTION of the trenches astride the La Bassee road. Hd. Qr. 7 HARLEY ST. D Coy in Company right in the front & support line A & C the left. B, C, & D in the night. 1 Coy of Middlesex remain in local reserve behind us. Relief completed at 8.30 pm	

(73989) W4141—463. 400,000. 9/14. H.&J.Ltd. Forms/C. 2118/10.

WAR DIARY or INTELLIGENCE SUMMARY.

Army Form C. 2118.

(Erase heading not required.)

Hour, Date, Place	Summary of Events and Information	Remarks and references to Appendices
TRENCHES. 22nd	The line we have to hold is badly cut up by craters, & it is a difficult line to hold	
24th	At 6.35 am the enemy sprang a mine in front of A Coy 20 yds from our mine, the men were at once occupied by Sr. Serjeant O 2 men & the connecting trench began manned with slight bombing.	
25th	Early in the morning about 2. a.m LIFISON J.R.L. Sjt. EVERED & a few men proceeded to attack the enemy who had 5 more occupied the furthest lip of the crater. It is believed the two of the enemy were killed & many injured by the grenades thrown & we consolidated the position on our side which had been lost on the previous day	

Army Form C. 2118.

WAR DIARY
or
INTELLIGENCE SUMMARY.
(Erase heading not required.)

Instructions regarding War Diaries and Intelligence Summaries are contained in F.S. Regs., Part II. and the Staff Manual respectively. Title pages will be prepared in manuscript.

Hour, Date, Place	Summary of Events and Information	Remarks and references to Appendices
TRENCHES. 27th MARCH.	The Battalion returned to ANNEQUIN NORTH they relieved by the 1/MIDDLESEX REGT. as before	
29th "	Regt is relieved by 2 Coys of MIDDLESEX REGT & 2 Coys of 4th Bn KINGS LIVERPOOL REGT. & return to billets at ECHOLE du JEUNES FILLES at BETHUNE	
BETHUNE 30th	Clean up & drills.	
31st	Lt Col TURNER addresses the Battalion on parade at 11 a.m afterwards inspecting it.	

98th Brigade.

33rd Division.

1/4th BATTALION

THE SUFFOLK REGIMENT

APRIL 1916

1/4 Suffolks

Army Form C. 2118.

WAR DIARY
or
INTELLIGENCE SUMMARY.
(Erase heading not required.)

Instructions regarding War Diaries and Intelligence Summaries are contained in F.S. Regs., Part II. and the Staff Manual respectively. Title pages will be prepared in manuscript.

1916

Hour, Date, Place		Summary of Events and Information	Remarks and references to Appendices
BETHUNE	April 1st	Heavy shell fire during night (3rd & 1st) Companies went for route marches	
	2nd	9.15am Divine Service at Theatre attended by Gen LANDON (G.O.C. 33rd Div") Received orders to dig trenches and erect gallows for Bayonet Fighting School at VENDIN. Moved at 2.15 pm to ANNEZIN taking over billets from 6th Scottish Rifles.	
ANNEZIN	3rd	COs Conference at Brigade Hd Qrs (10 AM) Company training continued	
	4th	Companies inspected by G.O.C. 98th Infantry Bde.	
	5th	Company training continued	
	6th	Address to Officers of 98th Infantry Bde at the Municipal Theatre BETHUNE by Lt Gen Haking K.C.B. (Corps Commander) The General laid stress on the importance of reducing the	

(73989) W4141—463. 400,000. 9/14. H.&J.Ltd. Forms/C. 2118/10.

Army Form C. 2118.

WAR DIARY
or
INTELLIGENCE SUMMARY.
(Erase heading not required.)

Instructions regarding War Diaries and Intelligence Summaries are contained in F.S. Regs., Part II. and the Staff Manual respectively. Title pages will be prepared in manuscript.

Hour, Date, Place		Summary of Events and Information	Remarks and references to Appendices
ANNEZIN	April 6th	Moral of the enemy and improving our own by raiding the enemy's trenches.	
	7th	Gas helmet drill by all Companies	
	8th	Company training continued	
	9th	Practice bomb raids	
	10th	Left ANNEZIN and returned to l'ECOLE des JEUNES FILLES BETHUNE	
BETHUNE	April 11th 12th 13th	Route marches and practice at judging distances was carried out by men not engaged on working parties	
	14th	Relieved the 1st MIDDLESEX REGT at ANNEQUIN S.	
ANNEQUIN, S.	15th	Working parties under R.E.s carried out by the Battalion	
	16th	Relieved the 1st MIDDLESEX REGT in AUCHY RIGHT SECTOR. Order of trenches. Order of Companies left to right D.C.B. A Company in Support. HdQrs of Regiment in RAILWAY ALLEY.	

Army Form C. 2118.

WAR DIARY
or
INTELLIGENCE SUMMARY.
(Erase heading not required.)

Instructions regarding War Diaries and Intelligence Summaries are contained in F.S. Regs., Part II and the Staff Manual respectively. Title pages will be prepared in manuscript.

Hour, Date, Place		Summary of Events and Information	Remarks and references to Appendices
IN THE TRENCHES	April 19th 19th	Wet weather occasioned much repair to trenches. Wiring carried on nightly under difficulties as M.G. fire and rifle fire was heavy. A few casualties occurred wiring also rifle grenades were active. These we overcame returning 3 for every one.	
	20th	Relieved by 1st MIDDLESEX REGT and returned to ANNEQUIN S.	
ANNEQUIN S.	21st	Weather very bad. Working parties found for R.E.s	
	22nd	Relieved 1st MIDDLESEX REGT in AUCHY RIGHT Sector. Fine weather. Repairs to trenches continued by day and wiring by night.	
IN THE TRENCHES	23rd	Easter Sunday. HOLY DAY and were quietly disposed.	
	24th	A Quiet day in trenches. Work carried on improving same. The Germans displayed a notice "A MERRY	
	25th	Raiding party of 1st MIDDLESEX left our right company's lines at 10.0 pm and attacked enemy's lines at MAD POINT	

WAR DIARY
or
INTELLIGENCE SUMMARY.
(Erase heading not required.)

Army Form C. 2118.

Hour, Date, Place	Summary of Events and Information	Remarks and references to Appendices
IN THE TRENCHES. April 25th	After an intense bombardment. Raid was successful, three prisoners being captured. Casualties slight.	
26th	Relieved by 2nd Worcestershire Regt (100th Bde.) Regiment returned to ANNEZIN, arriving 2 am morning of 27th	
ANNEZIN 27th	7 am Poison gas came over from enemy attack on Loos Salient. This soon passed off	
28th	Cleaning up clothes and equipment. Company training	
29th	Genl Strickland C.M.G. D.S.O. and Col Rowley ofBrigadier inspected new draft and afterwards the companies at musketry instruction.	
30th	Church Parade. Address by our chaplain (Capt Stone.)	
May 1st	Brigade Route march via Ourleke - HINSETTE - HINGES - VENDIN - ANNEZIN. marching excellent. Only one sick man fell out. It was noted by the G.O.C. that some officer's chargers carried more fodder than others.	

98th Brigade.

33rd Division.

1/4th BATTALION

THE SUFFOLK REGIMENT

M A Y 1 9 1 6

Reports on Raid 13/14th Attached.

Army Form C. 2118.

WAR DIARY
or
INTELLIGENCE SUMMARY.
(Erase heading not required.)

Instructions regarding War Diaries and Intelligence Summaries are contained in F. S. Regs., Part II. and the Staff Manual respectively. Title pages will be prepared in manuscript.

Place	Date	Hour	Summary of Events and Information	Remarks and references to Appendices
	1st May 1916		Brigade route march via AVELETTE - HINSETTE - HINGES - VENDIN - ANNEZIN. Marching excellent Only one sick man fell out. It was noted by the G.O.C. that some officers chargers carried more fodder than others	

Army Form C. 2118.

WAR DIARY
or
INTELLIGENCE SUMMARY.
(Erase heading not required.)

Instructions regarding War Diaries and Intelligence Summaries are contained in F.S. Regs., Part II. and the Staff Manual respectively. Title pages will be prepared in manuscript.

Hour, Date, Place	Summary of Events and Information	Remarks and references to Appendices
ANNEZIN May 2nd	Company training continued. Improvements to Billets and drainage.	
3rd	Bayonet school visited by officers. Musketry range allotted to Battalion. Lecture on Courts Martial by Divisional General (Gen LANDON CB.)	
4th	Relieved the 2nd R.W. Fusiliers in CUINCHY RIGHT sector of the trenches. Order of Companies (left to right) D.C.B.A	
IN THE TRENCHES May 5th & 7th	Very quiet time except for hand grenade fighting in Craters. Wiring continued each night. Careful patrolling of enemy wire N. of BETHUNE – LA BASSÉE ROAD.	
8th	Relieved by 1st MIDDLESEX Regt and returned to ANNEQUIN N.	
ANNEQUIN N. May 9th & 10th	Working parties under R.E's. Billets whitewashed – Wash-houses built and general improvements to billets.	
11th	Working parties continued. 5.10 p.m. ANNEQUIN N. heavily shelled by 8" naval shell.	

WAR DIARY
or
INTELLIGENCE SUMMARY.

(Erase heading not required.)

Army Form C. 2118.

Hour, Date, Place	Summary of Events and Information	Remarks and references to Appendices
ANNEQUIN N. May 11th	Shell. Regiment had an unpleasant hour during the bombardment, but no casualties resulted.	
12th	Relieved 1st MIDDLESEX REGT in CUINCHY RIGHT Sector of the trenches. A quiet night. Gaps in enemy wire N. of LA BASSEE Rd	
IN THE TRENCHES May 13	At 1.30 am (on the morning of 13th–14th inst) a raid was carried out on the enemy lines N. of the BETHUNE – LA BASSEE Rd Copy of the official record attached.	
14th	At 6.35 pm the enemy sprung a mine about 40 yards from our right company fire trench. Enemy occupied same but was immediately driven out. Saps were dug to craters during the night and craters consolidated. German prisoner officer was captured in Crater (2nd Lieut 2nd Res Regt Saxon) Official account (copy) attached.	
15th	A quiet day in trenches. Work carried on by night improving approaches to (14/5/16) Crater. This was officially named	

Army Form C. 2118.

WAR DIARY
or
INTELLIGENCE SUMMARY.
(Erase heading not required.)

Instructions regarding War Diaries and Intelligence Summaries are contained in F.S. Regs., Part II. and the Staff Manual respectively. Title pages will be prepared in manuscript.

Hour, Date, Place	Summary of Events and Information	Remarks and references to Appendices
IN THE TRENCHES		
May 15th IPSWICH Crater		
	10 pm A British mine was sprung under hostile sap. Front line and support lines in right company were vacated to prevent loss of life from falling debris	
	11 pm Hostile bombardment following mine explosion ceased and working parties were able to continue on IPSWICH Crater	
	3 am British mine sprung by regiment on our left in CUINCHY left sector.	
16th	Relieved by 1st MIDDLESEX Regt. Regiment returns to billets in ANNEQUIN N.	
ANNEQUIN N. May 17th to 19th.	Working parties under R.E.s. Gas helmet drill. Improvements carried out in billets	

Army Form C. 2118.

WAR DIARY
OR
INTELLIGENCE SUMMARY.
(Erase heading not required.)

4th SUFFOLK REGIMENT.

Hour, Date, Place	Summary of Events and Information	Remarks and references to Appendices
ANNEQUIN NORTH May 20th IN THE TRENCHES. 21st 22nd 23rd 24th	Relieved 1st MIDDLESEX REGT in CUINCHY RIGHT SECTOR of the trenches. Order of Companys (left to Right) D.B.C.A. Communication to left company very bad owing to recent trench mortar bombardment by the enemy. Fine weather. Work carried out cleaning trenches in left Company's front, deepening and revetting front line. Strengthening sapheads. Major COPEMAN H.C. D.S.O (R.F.O) 9th ESSEX REGT assumes command of the Battalion. Heavy bombardment of the enemy's front line system by our artillery at 4.30 pm 10.30 pm midnight (23rd 24th) and 2.15 am. Considerable damage was done to the enemy's defences. Our snipers were active firing on enemy seen through gaps in enemy parapet. 4.30 – 6.30 pm enemy bombarded left company's front and support lines, also reserve lines intensively. Front line was	

Army Form C. 2118.

WAR DIARY
or
INTELLIGENCE SUMMARY.
(Erase heading not required.)

4th SUFFOLK REGIMENT.

Instructions regarding War Diaries and Intelligence Summaries are contained in F.S. Regs., Part II. and the Staff Manual respectively. Title pages will be prepared in manuscript.

Hour, Date, Place	Summary of Events and Information	Remarks and references to Appendices
IN THE TRENCHES. May 24th	Cleared, part sheltering in deep dug-outs and part in tops. The tops being very near to hostile lines were free from bombardment, and by manning them we were able to keep a look-out for any infantry attack by the enemy. The result of this action was that only two casualties resulted. Relieved by 1st Middlesex Regt and returned to billets at Annequin North.	
ANNEQUIN NORTH. May 25th to May 26th	Working parties continued day and night in 8 hour shifts under 251st Tunnelling Coy R.E. Working party also found to repair front line damaged in enemy bombardment of May 24th. All other available men employed improving billets. A large quantity of government property discovered in French woman's house. Matter reported to A.P.M. and property recovered. 3 p.m. Billets inspected by G.O.C. 98th Bde. 5 p.m. Orders received cancelling relief of 98th Bde. as arranged for the following day by the 100th Bde.	
28th	Working parties under 251st Tunnelling Coy R.E. continued. Orders received at 3 p.m. that Bde would be relieved same night by 116th & 17th Bde	

(73989) W4141—463. 400,000. 9/14. H.&J.Ltd. Forms/C. 2118/10.

Army Form C. 2118.

WAR DIARY
or
INTELLIGENCE SUMMARY.
(Erase heading not required.)

4th SUFFOLK REGIMENT

Instructions regarding War Diaries and Intelligence Summaries are contained in F.S. Regs., Part II and the Staff Manual respectively. Title pages will be prepared in manuscript.

Hour, Date, Place		Summary of Events and Information	Remarks and references to Appendices
ANNEQUIN NORTH. May 28th		Relieved by 12th B.n Sussex Regt at 11.0 p.m. and return to Billets at L'Ecole De Jeunes Filles.	
BETHUNE.	29th	Receive orders to be prepared to move on short notice. Cleaning up equipment etc inspected and deficiencies made good. C.O. and 2 Company Commanders reconnoitre the approaches to the 15th & 16th Divisional Front.	
	30th	Two Company Commanders reconnoitre approaches to 1st Divisional Front. Reveille 5.30 a.m. Physical Drill 7 - 7.45 a.m. 9am to 12.45 p.m. and 2.0 p.m. to 3.30 p.m. Bayonet fighting, Bomb throwing and company training.	
	31st	C.O. and 2 Company Commanders reconnoitre 1st Divisional Front. Company training continued, including instruction and practice in wiring. Lectures on sanitation and gas helmets drill.	
June.	1st	Training continued.	
	2nd	Divisional Order received notifying the following awards. Capt. Burges R. } awarded the D.S.O. Lieut. Bond. A.J. " Hume. R.D. } the Military Cross " Jeson. G.F.L.	

(73989) W4141—463. 400,000. 9/14. H.&J.Ltd. Forms/C. 2118/10.

Capture of crater by 1/4th Suffolk Regiment.

To:- G.O.C., 98th Infantry Brigade.

The enemy sprung a mine about 6.35 p.m. at A.21.d.67.09. The crater is about 25 yards across, and there is a space of about 10 yards between this crater and NEW CRATER A.21.d.86.13.

A party of the enemy about 20 strong at once rushed to occupy the crater, apparently from the crater at A.21.d.75.08. They could be seen from the sap to MARCH CRATER, and rapid fire was immediately opened on them.

At this time and during subsequent operations at least 12 of the enemy were killed or wounded (including an Officer) by rifle fire.

A party of 7 of these succeeded in getting into the crater and occupied the western lip, from which they threw bombs at our front line. All their bombs fell a few yards short.

At the same time an artillery barrage was placed along HIGH STREET, BACK STREET, and TOWER RESERVE TRENCH. We asked for artillery retaliation, which was given at once and was very effective. When the enemy fire quietened down our artillery also ceased.

Immediately it was seen that the enemy had occupied the crater snipers were posted at all points of vantage, notably at the junction of the sap to NEW CRATER with the main sap. These snipers very successfully kept down all sniping from the crater.

Stokes T.M.B. also fired on the crater. Several Mills Grenades were also thrown in by the best long-range thrower in the Battalion.

At dusk, after rapid fire by the Stokes Mortar, and a few rounds by the 2" Mortar T.33 T.M.B., a party consisting of 1 Officer, 5 Bombers, and 6 bayonet men with shovels rushed the near lip of the crater from a sap leading to New Crater, but found that the enemy had fled, leaving one very badly wounded man. It was thought that the enemy could be heard on their lip of the crater, notwithstanding this L/Cpl. Webb at once went into the crater and with help brought the German out.

Work was at once commenced on sapping as per attached plan.

The crater was thoroughly examined later, and it was found that the enemy had cut 7 small one-man platforms into the western lip. Several spades and bags of bombs were brought back, and the wounded man's rifle.

A plan for attacking the enemy on his lip of the crater was formed, but an Officer's Patrol which worked round inside the lip of the crater discovered that the enemy had abandoned the eastern lip also, and no signs of sapping could be seen.

The enemy was very much alert, and spotted the patrol as soon as their heads were raised above the lip of the crater, and opened rifle and M.G. fire.

The personal effects of the wounded German are sent herewith. There is no chance of his recovery.

The board with the paper on it was stuck in the western lip of the crater, so that the side on which the paper was faced the enemy line. It was obviously a guide for enemy artillery and trench mortar fire.

With reference to the work in progress on attached sketch. All saps shown have been dug sufficiently deep to afford cover.

Wire has been put out to the south of the new sap as shown, but it was found impossible, owing to enemy fire and bombs to carry out the wiring in front of the T head that covers the gap between New Crater and the Crater of 14/5/16. Wire balls will be prepared and put out.

The following telegram has been received:-
"Corps and Divisional Commanders wire congratulations for prompt action at new crater, especially in view of opposition."

(sd) F.V. Turner, Lieut.Col.
Comdg. 1/4th Suffolk Regt..

15/5/16.

Raid by the 1/4th Suffolk Regt.,
on the night of 13/14th May, 1916.

The two parties, each consisting of 1 Officer, 1 Sergeant, and 9 Other Ranks, advanced simultaneously towards the two gaps. As they advanced, three shots were fired in the air, apparently from the sniper's post.

As the front men reached the parapet, the parties were met with a shower of bombs. They rushed forward to get into the trench, but found it covered over except for a few spaces about 2 feet wide and about 20 feet apart. Between the wire and the trench was a ditch about 2 feet deep and about 3 feet wide. From the bottom of this the parapet stood up about 2 feet, and on getting over this they found themselves in what seemed like very soft soil at the same level as the top of the parapet, and beyond this again and on the same level were what appeared to be boards covering the trench below; then came about 2 feet of level, and then the parados, which was about a foot higher; and in a mound rising out of this, and facing the gaps, was a sniper's plate, from which 3 shots were fired before he was silenced by our bombs and revolver shots. There is little doubt that these 3 shots killed our 3 missing men, or at any rate two of them, who were seen lying close together on or near the parapet, and who were the leading men.

The enemy's bombs were thrown from the holes in the covering over the trench, and were landed with great accuracy in the two gaps in the wire.

Capt. Brunger got through one of these holes on to the fire-step in the trench, whilst Sergt. Feaden fired 3 shots into another; Sergt. Woodard fired 6 and Cpl. Dodd 6 into another.

Lieut Hume threw 3 bombs into one, and Pte. Mason threw one into another. Cries and groans were heard from below the boarding, and the number of casualties must have been large.

Seeing there was no chance of getting into the trench and carrying out the intentions of the raid, Capt. Brunger blew his whistle and the party retired, the only casualty during retirement being one man wounded by a rifle shot as he got into the crater.

The total casualties were three men missing (probably killed), two men severely wounded, and one Officer and 4 men slightly wounded.

The following telegram has been received:-
"Divisional Commander appreciates the spirit and resource shown by the raiding party of 'I.T.' under most difficult circumstances, and wishes all ranks to be so informed."

(sd) D.T.Turner, Lieut. Col.,
Comdg. 1/4th Suffolk Regt.

17/5/16.

98th Brigade.

33rd Division.

1/4th BATTALION

THE SUFFOLK REGIMENT

JUNE 1916

Entries for June 1st & 2nd will be found in War Diary for May 1916.

Army Form C. 2118.

WAR DIARY
or
INTELLIGENCE SUMMARY.
(Erase heading not required.)

4th SUFFOLK REGIMENT

Instructions regarding War Diaries and Intelligence Summaries are contained in F.S. Regs. Part II and the Staff Manual respectively. Title pages will be prepared in manuscript.

Hour, Date, Place	Summary of Events and Information	Remarks and references to Appendices
BETHUNE June 2nd	2064 Sergt Everad H 1574 2/Cpl Watt G. 1531 Sergt Woodard F. 1654 L/Sgt Beaton W. } awarded the Military Medal for...	
	A draft of 12 men returned to the Regt and 61 from the 31st Suffolks Regt arrive at Bethune.	
3rd	Company training continued. Particular attention is paid to Bayonet fighting. The D.C.M. awarded to 11.0 Coy Sgt Major Walker W. the Military Medal to 2056 Sgt Curran J.R.	
4th	Draft of six officers arrive. Company training continued.	
5th	Draft of two officers arrive.	
6th	Company training.	
7th	Company training. In the evening the 98th Infy Bde. held a concert at the Municipal Theatre, Bethune. 2nd Lieut Hooper, 2nd Lieut Knowlson and Pte Aldrich assisted to produce an excellent entertainment.	
8th	Company training continued. In the evening a Brigade Boxing Competition took place. Several NCOs and men put up an excellent fight.	
9th	Company training continued.	

Army Form C. 2118.

WAR DIARY
or
INTELLIGENCE SUMMARY.
(Erase heading not required.)

4th SUFFOLK REGIMENT

Hour, Date, Place	Summary of Events and Information	Remarks and references to Appendices
BETHUNE June 10th.	General Strickland Ch.S. D.S.O. bids farewell to the Officers of 98th Infy Bde on being appointed to the command of the 1st Division. In addressing the officers of the Regt. he spoke highly of the work the 4th Suffolk's had done not only in the 98th Bde but also while under his command in the Jullundur Bde.	
7.30 pm	Handed over billets to 6th Bn Warwickshire Regt. and marched to Annequin North where we relieved the 13th Bn Sussex Regt.	
ANNEQUIN NORTH. 1.0 am 11th.	Continuous working parties found for work under direction of 2.51st Tunnelling Coy R.E. and 11th Field Coy R.E.	
4.30 pm	Working party found for work on advanced Brigade HQrs.	
8.0 pm	Lt. Col. Copeman D.S.O. assumes temporary command of 98th Infy Bde, while awaiting the arrival of the new Brigadier.	
12th.	Working parties continued. Training continued in musketry. Wash-houses and field ovens built. Approaches to billets improved. General F.M. Carleton D.S.O. arrives at 98th Bde HQrs. and assumes command.	

Army Form C. 2118.

WAR DIARY
or
INTELLIGENCE SUMMARY.
(Erase heading not required.)

4th SUFFOLK REGIMENT.

Hour, Date, Place	Summary of Events and Information	Remarks and references to Appendices
ANNEQUIN. NORTH. June 13th.	Baths at Annequin are under repair and consequently are not available for use. A change of underclothing for all ranks however is obtained. Working parties continued under very bad weather conditions. N.C.O.s and men continue to attend Divisional Classes of instruction.	
14th	Working parties continued. 11.0 p.m. time advanced 1 hour (Daylight Saving.)	
15th	Officers (Company Commanders) visit GIVENCHY SECTOR. Left Sub. Section.	
16th	C.O. and Adjt. visit the line Regt. is taking over the following day. The following officers and warrant officers were mentioned in Sir Douglas Haig's despatch dated.	
	Lieut. (tempy Capt.) H. Pretty.	
	Tempy Lieut. F.C.C. Tyson. (in command of Tr. Mr. Battery.)	
	Lieut. J.G. Frere. (Suffolk Regt) seconded for duty with 11th Suffolk Regt.	
	54.0. C.S.Major W. Finch.	
	Working parties under R.E. continued till 6 p.m.	
17th	Lewis Gunners, Snipers, Observers and Bombers relieve 1st Herts Regt and	

WAR DIARY
or
INTELLIGENCE SUMMARY.
(Erase heading not required.)

Army Form C. 2118.

4th SUFFOLK REGIMENT

Hour, Date, Place	Summary of Events and Information	Remarks and references to Appendices
ANNEQUIN NORTH. June 17th.	One Company of 6th Cheshire Regt. also 1st Cambridgeshire Regt. (1 platoon in Keep) 118th Bde. by daylight in the Givenchy Sector. Left Sub-section. The relief of rifles was carried out after dark and completed at 12.30 (14th-18th). Hostile rifle grenades active for ½ an hour then quiet. Our billets at Annequin North were handed over to the 18th Middlesex Regt. (Pioneer Battalion) 33rd Division - relief of the first ½ an hour then	
IN THE TRENCHES. June 18th. GIVENCHY SECTOR LEFT SUBSECTION.	The line we took over was apportioned to Companies as follows :- Right "A" Coy Right Centre "B" Coy Left Centre "C" Coy Left "D" Coy. There was much work required thickening and heightening breastworks, building parados, which in places were non existent. Also there was a quantity of unserviceable trench stores and ammunition to salve. This work was carried on by day and wiring and strengthening of a number of sap-heads by night. A quiet day.	
19th	Line visited by R.W.F. 19th Bde at 3.0 p.m. R.E. exploded a small mine in front of "B" Coy line. At 8.10 p.m.	

WAR DIARY
or
INTELLIGENCE SUMMARY.
(Erase heading not required.)

Army Form C. 2118.

4th SUFFOLK REGIMENT

Hour, Date, Place	Summary of Events and Information	Remarks and references to Appendices
IN THE TRENCHES: June 19th	The lip of this was immediately seized and work commenced consolidating same. Little enemy activity at once, but between 10 pm and 11 pm enemy retaliated with considerable bombardment, artillery and meinenwerfers, from in "C" Coys support lines and "B" Coys front line buried. These were extracted after two hours work, alive and not seriously injured. One sap held by "B" Coy and a portion of their front line badly blown in, causing a heavy nights work clearing same.	
20th 3.30 am	R.E. exploded a large mine in front of A & B Companies. The lip of this crater was immediately seized and held by the same party as the one the preceeding evening under 2nd Lt. Dooley W. Work immediately commenced consolidating crater lip and sapping out to same. Considerable hostile meinenwerfer activity on front line and artillery fire on support lines and keeps.	
21st	Enemy bombarded "B" and "F" lines heavily between 9.0 am and 11.0 am	

(73989) W4141—463. 400,000. 9/14. H.&J.Ltd. Forms/C. 2118/10.

Army Form C. 2118.

WAR DIARY
or
INTELLIGENCE SUMMARY.
(Erase heading not required.)

4th SUFFOLK REGIMENT.

Hour, Date, Place	Summary of Events and Information	Remarks and references to Appendices
IN THE TRENCHES June 21st	Work repairing and revetting Sap and Front line trenches continued till relieved by 1st Royal Welsh Fusiliers. This relief was completed about 12.30 (21st/22nd). 1½ hours before the enemy exploded a series of very heavy mines on the right Companies front of R.W. Fusiliers. (The Fusiliers suffered heavy casualties, but successfully drove the enemy — who had entered their trenches — out. In addition to casualties outside the enemy left 9 dead and one wounded man in the British trenches.) Regt. returned to billets taking over from the R.W.F. at Gorre. Two Companies and HQrs at Gorre Chateau, two Companies in farm buildings	
Gorre. June 22nd	Cleaning up and indenting for clothing and equipment. Revd F. Stone (Chaplain) bids us farewell on his appointment as senior Chaplain 4.0th Division	
23rd	5.30 am to 10 pm. ten different working parties numbering 300 men in all found for work under R.E. in trenches. 4.30 pm Heavy thunderstorm. Draft 2 Officer reinforcements join Batt" Lt. (Temp Capt.) Turner A.K. and 2nd Lt. Sykes C.Y.	

Army Form C. 2118.

WAR DIARY
or
INTELLIGENCE SUMMARY.
(Erase heading not required.)

4th Suffolk Regt.

Hour, Date, Place 1916	Summary of Events and Information	Remarks and references to Appendices
GORRE June 24th	Draft. Re-inforcements duty joined. Lieut. Bryant 1 Officer Capt B. Lt J. Glanfield (rejoined) 2 R.S.O's 6 men T.R.W.R. 2nd Lieut. Arnold of The following extract appeared in London Gazette dated 3.6.16 No 11940. C.S.M. Walker W. awarded Distinguished Conduct Medal " 2056 Sergt Ennion J. " Military Medal.	
25th (Sunday)	Rev. C. J. Kendall (New Chaplain) holds services for 'A' and 'B' Coys in Chateau and for 'C' & 'D' Coys at their respective billets.	
26th	C.O. holds a conference of all officers at 10 am. Parades. Skirmishing. Loading and firing practice in Gas Helmets. Inspection of Rifles by Armourer Sergeant. G.O.C. inspects the Battalion at work. Capt B. Lt J. Glanfield appointed 2nd in Command from 26.6.16 Capt Harold Pretty assumes command of 'B' Coy from 26.6.16	
27th	Brigade Route march via LE. HAMEL - ESSARS - S. bank of Canal to GORRE Draft Reinforcements. 45 men report to Unit at 4.15 pm Heavy rainfall at night.	
28th	Parade Ground too wet for drill. Inspection of Draft by C.O. Bombing. Wiring instruction, Gas Helmet Drill Parade.	

R.W. Glanfield. Capt.

Army Form C. 2118.

WAR DIARY
or
INTELLIGENCE SUMMARY.

(Erase heading not required.)

11th Suffolk Regt

Hour, Date, Place	Summary of Events and Information	Remarks and references to Appendices
GORRE June 29th	Parades, musketry, Trench duties, Bayonet fighting. Capt. H.K. TURNER assumes command of "C" Coy from 23-6-16.	
June 30th	Parade in afternoon :— A&D Coys carry out Outpost scheme. C&B " firing at ANNEZIN Range.	

98th Inf.Bde.
33rd Div.

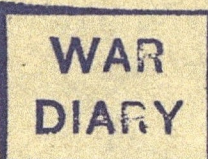

1/4th BATTN. THE SUFFOLK REGIMENT.

J U L Y

1 9 1 6

Attached:

Appendix "A".

Army Form C. 2118.

F.M.C.
F.

1/4th Suffolk Regt

WAR DIARY
or
INTELLIGENCE SUMMARY.
(Erase heading not required.)

1st R. Hereford. Regt

Hour, Date, Place	Summary of Events and Information	Remarks and references to Appendices

July 1st

C.O. and Company Commanders go up to line at CUINCHY Left. Sub Section and are promise to be taken over on relieving 16th K.R.R.C. in Bn Reserve
Gr of Winson B & C Coys carry out Outpost Scheme. A & D " firing a Range in GORRE 10700(B90)

July 2nd (Sunday)

Church Parade for A & B Coys in Courtyard of Chateau and ditional for C & D Coys.
Court of Enquiry held at H.Q. to deal with letter from Base Paymaster re old Pay a/c's. President Capt. B.S.I. Glanfield — Members Capt H Ruby and Capt H.G. King.
All Kits packed and transport and workshops moved to BEUVRY.
Battn moved at 16 Brigade Reserve via ANNEQUIN by platoons, the leading platoon of B Coy moving at 8.45 p.m.
Guides met platoons 1/2m at ANNEQUIN Cross Road. Battn reported as having completely taken over Reserve Line, with H.Q. at WIMPOLE STREET at 1.30 am 3.7.16 from 16th K.R.R.C.

J.R. Glanfield capt

Army Form C. 2118.

4th Suffolk Regt.

WAR DIARY
or
INTELLIGENCE SUMMARY.
(Erase heading not required.)

Hour, Date, Place	Summary of Events and Information	Remarks and references to Appendices
IN THE TRENCHES. July 3rd QUINCHY. Left Sub-Section.	Battn holding Reserve Line trenches Bryant 1 - 20. "A" Coy on Right with Coy HQ. in Factory Lane "D" " " Left " " " - Cambrin Support.	B.sgt. Yempeld Capt.

WAR DIARY

INTELLIGENCE SUMMARY

1/4th Suffolk Regt

Army Form C. 2118.

Hour, Date, Place	Summary of Events and Information	Remarks and references to Appendices
July 3rd & 6th	Battalion in VILLAGE LINE, CURLU Section. Working parties furnished for 251st Tunnelling Coy. R.E.; and for H⁴ King's in front line. Trenches, dug outs, and keeps maintained and repaired.	
July 4	The 9/8th Bn. are relieved by 11/6th Bn. and 13th Bn. (Rifles) Generalin relieved 1/4 Suffolks, etc. proceeded to BELLERIVE.	
July 8	The Bn. took over billets at BELLERIVE at 6 a.m. Orders received to entrain at CHOQUES or 9th Transport and loading parties were sent forward.	
July 9	The Bn. paraded at 1.45 a.m. and marched to CHOQUES Station, entraining there at 4 a.m. Detrained at AMIENS, and marched to RAINNEVILLE, where billets were taken over at 6 p.m. Rested and cleaned billets.	
July 10	Moved at 6.10 a.m. and marched to VAUX-SUR-SOMME, arriving there at 3 p.m., and taking over billets in huts in WELLCOME WOOD.	
July 11		

B.G. Turner
Lt. Col.

WAR DIARY
INTELLIGENCE SUMMARY
(Erase heading not required.)

Army Form C. 2118.

1/4th Suffolk Regt

Hour, Date, Place	Summary of Events and Information	Remarks and references to Appendices
July 12th	The Battn. paraded at 9 p.m. and marched to VILLE-SOUS-CORBIE with 4th Kings Regt. as left Column under Lt Col Copeman D.S.O. Here the Bn Bivouacked. Capt. H.V.Duke and 2/Lts EATON & SOTTIE joined Bn.	
July 13th. 10.30pm	Marched to MÉAULTE, and took over billets. Orders received to be ready to turn out at 2½ an hours notice.	
July 14th	Left MÉAULTE at 11.0.am. and marched to BÉCORDEL. At 4 p.m. the Battn moved to a position EAST of FRICOURT, where they bivouacked.	
July 15th. 6.0 am	The Battn moved to support Switch Trench. Regt. as for attack formed the first line, and 'C' & 'D' 'A' & 'B' Coys the second. A line immediately in front of the village of BAZENTIN LE PETIT was eventually taken up and held throughout the day	

WAR DIARY
INTELLIGENCE SUMMARY

Army Form C. 2118.

1/4th Suffolk Regt.

Hour, Date, Place	Summary of Events and Information	Remarks and references to Appendices
15th July	The casualties in the Battalion were heavy, and included the following:— Capt M.A Turner, Capt H.K Turner, 2nd Lieuts W.H. Milburn and W.H. Packard, killed Capt H. Pretty, 2nd Lieuts D H Pilkington, H. Scrimgeour, N H Smith, T.C.H Woods, H.F Bond, W.J. Dooley, E.J. Harding, G E E Burton, A.E. Moorsom, wounded. C.S.M. Walker. killed C.S.M's Roach, Scroggins, and Ives, wounded.	⊕ Died 16/7/16 ⊕ Died 19/7/16

WAR DIARY
or
INTELLIGENCE SUMMARY.

Army Form C. 2118

11th Suffolk Regt.

Hour, Date, Place	Summary of Events and Information	Remarks and references to Appendices
July 16th	During the early morning the Bn was relieved by the 2nd Bn A. & S.H., and went into Reserve at "Shell Valley" S.E. of BAZENTIN-le-PETIT, where the Bn dug itself in, and remained for the night.	
July 17th	Improvement of Reserve trench continued. A platoon of the 160th Inf. Regt was captured in a clump dug-out in the valley. Orders were received that the 33rd Divn. should attack SWITCH TRENCH, but these were afterwards cancelled, and at 11:30 p.m. the Bn moved off to relieve the 10th K.O.Y.L.I. in the front line. Heavy shelling experienced throughout the day.	
July 18th	Relief of 10th K.O.Y.L.I. completed at about 5:0 a.m. Headquarters established in old German bomb-store in N.E. corner of BAZENTIN le PETIT Wood.	

Army Form C. 2118.

1/4th Suffolk Regt.

WAR DIARY
INTELLIGENCE SUMMARY.
(Erase heading not required.)

Hour, Date, Place	Summary of Events and Information	Remarks and references to Appendices
July 19th.	Heavy hostile shelling on all fronts during the day. C.O. and Coy Comdrs of L.N.Lancs Regt visited line.	
July 20th.	The Batn were relieved by the L.N.Lancs. 56th Inf Bde, and retired to "Shell Valley" where improvement on trenches were continued. At 7 am indications were received to have in a position in the 19th Inf Bde in support of the 19th Inf Bde in an attack on HIGH WOOD and a German Trench N. of same. D Coy was first sent forward, the remaining Coys taking shelter & digging in. D Coy, with Battn HQ & 2" Trenches attempted to take a German switch point, but this effort was held up by heavy M.G. fire, and the Coy blind to await darkness. At about 4.30 pm., A & B Coys, under L. BROWN, were sent forward, but they also were compelled to retire. Lieut G.A.C. GOODALL was killed, and 2nd Lt. TURNER, L. EATON and Lt PATTISSON wounded.	[signature] Lieut and Adjt

Army Form C. 2118.

1/4th Suffolk Regt

WAR DIARY
INTELLIGENCE SUMMARY.
(Erase heading not required.)

Hour, Date, Place	Summary of Events and Information	Remarks and references to Appendices
July 21st	The Battn. was relieved by the WORCESTER SHIRE Regt., and proceeded to MAMETZ WOOD, and bivouacked. At about 8 p.m. orders were received that the Battn. would be relieved and march to DERNANCOURT. During the afternoon and night the wood was heavily shelled with H.E., shrapnel, and tear & gas shells.	
July 22nd	At about 1 a.m. the 4th Suffolk Regt. was relieved by the 6th Black Watch, and marched to DERNANCOURT, where billets were taken over at 5.0 a.m. Reinforcement of 983 Other Ranks joined the Battn. here.	
July 23rd to 31st	The Battalion rested in billets at DERNANCOURT, and refitting and training were carried on. The Battn. was inspected by the G.O.C. The following officers joined the Battn. from England. 2nd Lieut. C.P. PARRY-CROOKE, H.W. WOODS, E. NORTON, I. RHYS-JONES, K.C. SHUTTLEWORTH, E.G. JOYCE, C.C.S. GIBBS, A.C. PAWSEY. Major F. PRETTY joined Battn. from England 23-7-16	

APPENDIX "A".

1/4th Bn Suffolk Regt

Apendix "A"

Casualties during July

Date & month	Officers			O.Ranks		
	Killed	Wounded	Missing	Killed	Wounded	Missing
1st ~ 14th nil.						
July 15th	5	11	–	23	146	17
16th	–	–	–	2	11	–
17th	–	–	–	.	4	–
18th	–	1		.	5	1
19th	–	–	–	1	10	.
20th	1	3	–	14	79	20
21st ~ 31st nil.						
Total.	6	15	–	40	255	38

R.W. Turner
Lt. Adjt
1/4th Suffolk Regt.

(98th Brigade.
33rd Division.

1/4th BATTALION

SUFFOLK REGIMENT

AUGUST 1916.

Army Form C. 2118.

WAR DIARY
or
INTELLIGENCE SUMMARY.
(Erase heading not required.)

1/4th Suffolk Regiment

Vol II

Hour, Date, Place	Summary of Events and Information	Remarks and references to Appendices
Tuesday Aug 1st DERNANCOURT	Horton day. Parades were dismissed at 11:30 am and a half holiday was granted by the C.O. A number of Officers and men proceeded to MERICOURT on the invitation of the 2nd Suffolk Regt, who were resting there, and took part in a return polo match and other sports, and were most hospitably entertained. Major E.P. CLARKE assumed the duties of Staff Captain 98th Inf. Bde.	
Wednesday Aug 2nd	Training carried on. 2nd Lieut H.W. WOODS went to hospital. A lecture by Capt MYRES R.F.C. to all Officers by the Brigade at his Headquarters on the subject of contact aeroplane patrol signalling. Orders received to be ready to move at 24hrs notice. Training carried on.	
Thursday Aug 3rd		
Friday Aug 4th	Training continued with night operations. The Officers entertained a party of Officers from the 2nd Suffolk Regt who came over from MERICOURT to dinner.	

F. Pretty
1/4 Suffolk Regt

WAR DIARY
or
INTELLIGENCE SUMMARY.

Army Form C. 2118.

4/14th Bn Suffolk Regt.

Hour, Date, Place	Summary of Events and Information	Remarks and references to Appendices
Saturday Aug 5	The C.O. and Boy Corporal visited Fricourt area, and looked over the trenches, etc, to be taken over by the battalion.	
Sunday Aug 6	Reg. holiday in the afternoon. Church Parade at 10.0 am. The Battalion moved at 3.20 pm to the Fricourt Area. Rd Seaforth Rig Dunan. Bn Ches from H.Q. Headquarters and A, B, & C Coys along the edge of Fricourt Wood and D Boy in cellars in Fricourt village. Relief completed at 6 pm.	
Monday Aug 7	The battalion furnished a working party of H.H.Q. (110 from each Coy), under 219 Boy R.E. for digging "THISTLE ALLEY" communication trench. This party was subjected to considerable hostile shelling. Casualties 1 OR killed, and 2/Lt C.G. SYKES and 9 OR wounded	F. Prethkeyn Lt.Col. 1/4 Suffolk Regt

Army Form C. 2118.

WAR DIARY
or
INTELLIGENCE SUMMARY.
(Erase heading not required.)

1/4th Bn Suffolk Regt

Hour, Date, Place	Summary of Events and Information	Remarks and references to Appendices
Tuesday Aug 8th FRICOURT	Working Party of 200 for entrenching of THISTLE ALLEY supplied to 212th Coy R.E. from A & C Coys at 8 p.m.	
Wed. Aug 9th	Working parties supplied to 212th Coy as follows:— 8.0 am 200 men from B & D Coys. 8.0 pm 200 " " A & C " These were employed on THISTLE ALLEY, as before.	
Thurs. Aug 10th	Working parties of 200 from B & D Coys at 8.0 am; and 200 from A & C at 8 pm were furnished as on 9th.	
Friday Aug 11th	Working parties of 200 from B & D Coys at 8.0 am and 200 from A & C at 9.0 pm under 212th Coy R.E. for digging communication trenches.	

F. Pretty Major
1/4 Suffolk Regt

Army Form C. 2118.

WAR DIARY
or
INTELLIGENCE SUMMARY.
(Erase heading not required.)

1/4th Bn Suffolk Regt

Instructions regarding War Diaries and Intelligence Summaries are contained in F. S. Regs., Part II and the Staff Manual respectively. Title pages will be prepared in manuscript.

Hour, Date, Place	Summary of Events and Information	Remarks and references to Appendices
Aug 12 (Sat.) FRICOURT.	At 4 am the C.O and Coy Commrs visited the line and looked over trenches to be taken over by the Battn.	
Aug 13th (Sunday)	Moved from FRICOURT WOOD at 4.30 am, and proceeded to the support trenches in BAZENTIN LE GRAND where we relieved the 9th Bn H.L.I. This was completed by 7.45 am. On the way some wagons the line of German 5.9"s but did not suffer any casualties. The remainder of the day and night were uneventful.	
Aug 14th Monday.	At 6.0 am we left the line in BAZENTIN LE GRAND and relieved the 4th Bn Kings Liverpool Regt in the front line, the relief being completed by about 9 am, the trenches occupied by us in the front line were known as SEAFORTH trench, and our local support trench as BLACK WATCH trench. The front was	F Pretty Major 1/4 Suffolk Regt

Army Form C. 2118.

WAR DIARY
or
INTELLIGENCE SUMMARY.
(Erase heading not required.)

14th Bn Suffolk Regt

Hour, Date, Place	Summary of Events and Information	Remarks and references to Appendices
Aug 15th (Tuesday)	About 1000 yds and from S.E. from HIGH WOOD D Coy on the right and A Coy the left in SEAFORTH Trench and B & C supporting them in BLACK WATCH Trench. Work was at once started improving these trench at night, and connecting A, B, C and D Coys to form new trench lay down to WORCESTER Trench in advance of SEAFORTH Trench.	
Aug 15th (Tuesday)	Much hard work put in by improving existing trenches and continuing WORCESTER Trench. The area was constantly shelled.	
Aug 16th (Wednesday)	Work continued by day and night under same conditions. During the night Capt H.N. DUKE and 2nd Lt SHUTTLEWORTH were wounded whilst working on WORCESTER Trench.	

F. Pretty Major
14th Suffolk Regt

Army Form C. 2118.

WAR DIARY
or
INTELLIGENCE SUMMARY.
(Erase heading not required.)

Hour, Date, Place	Summary of Events and Information	Remarks and references to Appendices
Aug 14th	Work continued, and shelling rather more severe. During the night Lieut & Adjt. R. W. Turner was wounded by a shell. Our artillery carried out heavy bombardment of enemy positions. The following officers reported for duty with the regt at "B" echelon :— 2nd Lieuts C. M. Oliver, L. P. Bennett, S. C. Williams, J. S. Menhinick, B. S. Evans, G. G. B. Bannerman, and C. A. Harris.	

F. Reeve Major
11th Suffolk Regt.

WAR DIARY or INTELLIGENCE SUMMARY

Army Form C. 2118.

11th Bn Suffolk Regt.

Hour, Date, Place	Summary of Events and Information	Remarks and references to Appendices
Aug 18th	Capt J.F.L. Dixon joined the regiment in the line about 11am and took over the duties of Adjutant. At 2.45 pm the German trenches opposite were attacked. The order of battle was:- D Coy on right and A on left, with C in support and B in reserve. The 2nd & 4th at the same time assaulted the German position on our left in HIGH WOOD and the 4th Kings Liverpool Regt the trenches on our right. The assault was carried out with determination. D and C Coys reached the German trenches and remained in them for some time. 2nd Lt. Y.L.S. BEDWELL, the only surviving officer, was killed in advancing the German line. Eventually they had to retire as they had not been reinforced and rifles were got into the German trench, and hostile bombing attacks were repulsed, but finally the trench had to be abandoned and the men withdrew to SEAFORTH	F. Pretyman Lt Col 11th Suffolk Regt

Army Form C. 2118.

WAR DIARY
or
INTELLIGENCE SUMMARY.
(Erase heading not required.)

1/4th Suffolk Regt

Hour, Date, Place	Summary of Events and Information	Remarks and references to Appendices
Aug 18 (con'd)	Trench. The two troops conducted themselves admirably. 2/Lieuts V.L.S. BEDWELL, H.C. PAWSEY, and C. NORTON were killed, and Capt. H.F. LING and 2/Lt. N.E. TUTTLE wounded. O.R. Casualties - killed 29, wounded 102, missing 50.	7. Pretty Maps 1/4th Suffolk Regt.

Army Form C. 2118.

WAR DIARY
or
INTELLIGENCE SUMMARY.
(Erase heading not required.)

1/4th Bn Suffolk Regt

Hour, Date, Place	Summary of Events and Information	Remarks and references to Appendices
Aug 19th (Saturday)	The regiment was relieved by the 9th Scottish Rifles in the early morning and moved to FRICOURT WOOD where they remained throughout the day. At 6.30 pm they proceeded to a camp N.E. of MÉAULTE. Chag to the MEAULTE- ALBERT road. Two new officers reported for duty with the regt, namely Capt. E.L.D. LAKE and 2/Lieut C.M. BYGATE.	
Aug 20 (Sunday)	Church Parade at 11.0 am and afternoon the men enjoyed a much needed rest.	
Aug 21 (Monday)	Baths, inspection of clothing, kit, and equipment. German aeroplane flew over the camp and round and dropped bombs, without however doing any damage to the regiment.	
Aug 22 (Tuesday)	Day was spent re-fitting. Draft of 108 h Co's. other ranks arrived.	

F. Pretty Major
1/4th Suffolk Regt

Army Form C. 2118.

11th Bn Suffolk Regt

WAR DIARY
or
INTELLIGENCE SUMMARY.
(Erase heading not required.)

Hour, Date, Place	Summary of Events and Information	Remarks and references to Appendices
Aug 23rd (Wednesday)	Refitting continued, and parades under Company arrangements. C.O. and Coy Officers went up the line and reconnoitred trenches with a view to getting through with parade emergencies. A working body of 60 men provided.	
Aug 24th (Thursday)	The Batn moved to FRICOURT WOOD at 1.15 pm, and furnished three working parties of 40 men each during the night.	
Aug 25th (Friday)	Moved to MONTAUBAN ALLEY at 2.30 pm, arriving at 5 pm, and relieved 2nd WORCESTER Regt as Bde Reserve. At 9 pm we moved up as Left Support Batn to trenches E. of BAZENTIN LE GRAND, arriving at 1 am. 2nd Lieut C. W. BOTTON joined the Regt.	7 Pretty bays 11th Suffolk Regt
Aug 26th (Saturday)	Remained for the same trenches; furnished working parties for 9th a & S.H. in front line, and supplied two working parties totalling 250.	

WAR DIARY or INTELLIGENCE SUMMARY

Army Form C. 2118.

1/4th Bn Suffolk Regt.

Hour, Date, Place	Summary of Events and Information	Remarks and references to Appendices
Aug 27th (Sunday)	Again found fatigue and ration parties for Bns. in Line, and a working party of 200 during the night. 91 O.R. joined the Battn. as reinforcement.	
Aug 28th (Monday)	Relieved the 9th C.o.L. Regt in TEA TRENCH and newly captured portion of WOOD LANE. Relief was carried out by B Coy in firing line, A in support, C in ORCHARD TRENCH and D in reserve at PONT St. 4 O.R. joined the Battn as reinforcement.	
Aug 29th (Tuesday)	ORCHARD TRENCH greatly shelled at intervals, Both were consolidated and strengthened during the day. Weather changed and became very wet (a heavy thunderstorm)	
Aug 30th (Wed)	At 6.30 am the Germans made a strong bombing attack up WOOD LANE, which was repulsed by B Coy. Our casualties during the day were very light. The enemy's heavy.	F. Pretty Major 1/4th Suffolk Regt.

WAR DIARY or INTELLIGENCE SUMMARY

1/4th Bn Suffolk Regt

Hour, Date, Place	Summary of Events and Information	Remarks and references to Appendices
Aug 20th (cont'd)	Artillery steadily shelled Support line and communication trenches especially from 9 to 4 pm when ORCHARD Trench was severely bombarded, causing a good many casualties including Capt. B.P.J. GRANFIELD and Lieut. C.W. BOTTON and 2nd Lt. M. Oliver (in Post St). Relief by 13th Middlesex Regt commenced. Owing to heavy rain and consequent condition of the relief was not completed till 8.40 am next morning.	
Aug 21st Thursday	The battalion on being relieved by 8 Mdx and MEAULTE Camp on high ground N of DERNANCOURT. During the shell in trenches & to 21st the casualties got four officers wounded and 19 OR killed, 23 wounded and 5 missing. Capt. B.B. NOBLE R.A.M.C (attached) returned to ORCHARD trench after the relief and was unfortunately wounded himself and had retreated.	F. Pretty Major 1/4th Suffolk Regt

1/4TH BN SUFFOLK REGT
List of Casualties for month of August

Date	Killed	Wounded	Mg & Kd	Missing
	1	10		
	1	10		
		3		
		4		
		1		
	1			
	1	22		
	3	8		
	1			
	33	108	17	23
	1			
		4		
		1		
		2		
	6	5	1	
	13	10	2	
		1		1
Totals	61	189	20	24

Officers

Date	Killed	Wounded
		2/Lt Sykes. G.G.
		2/Lt Shuttleworth. K.C.
		Capt Duke H.N.
	2/Lt Bedwell V.L.S.	Capt Ling H.T.
	--- Norton. E.	Lt. Turner K.W.
	--- Pawsey H.C	2/Lt Suttle. N.E.
		Capt Glanfield B St J
		~~2/Lt Norton E B~~
		2/Lt Oliver C.M
		--- Botton C.W.
		Capt Noble B.B. (RAMC)
Totals	3	10

J H Irwin
Capt & Adjt

98th Brigade.

33rd Division.

1/4th BATTALION

THE SUFFOLK REGIMENT

SEPTEMBER 1916

1/4th Bn Suffolk Regt
Casualties for September 1916

	Killed	Wounded
September 27th		1
28th	1	7
29th		
30th		1
Total	1	9

F. Pretty Major
for O.C. 1/4th Bn Suffolk Regt

Army Form C. 2118.

WAR DIARY
or
INTELLIGENCE SUMMARY.
(Erase heading not required.)

4th Bn Suffolk Regt.

Hour, Date, Place	Summary of Events and Information	Remarks and references to Appendices
Sept 25th	Digging working parties totaling 340 men. The following officers joined the Battalion:- Capt. F.S. Cubitt, 2nd Lieut. G.H.C. Adams, G.W.B. Hampton, H.H. Collis, G.S. Gough, E.G. Hannant, H.C. Hattam, C.A. Horton, H. Hoyland, S.B. Leader, K. Paterson, H.G. Topham, S.F. Thompson, S.H. Walker	
Sept. 26th	Moved into trenches in and East of HEBUTERNE and relieved the 1st Middlesex Regt. The relief was completed by 8.20 pm. We occupied the right of the RIGHT SECTOR. C. Coy on the right and D Coy on the left in front line, B Coy in support trenches, and A Coy in reserve in the village. Slight shelling from trench mortars during the night. Our patrols active. We established working parties totaling to 60 men from reserve Coy.	
Sept. 27th	Worked on improving line. Front line and village lightly and intermittently shelled during day. Casualty 1 OR wounded.	F. Brown Lt Col 4th Suffolk Regt.

Army Form C. 2118.

WAR DIARY
or
INTELLIGENCE SUMMARY.
(Erase heading not required.)

4th Bn Suffolk Regt

Hour, Date, Place	Summary of Events and Information	Remarks and references to Appendices
Sept. 28th	Worked on improving line. A quiet day except for a few trench mortars and light shells on our front line. About 10 pm 9 Germans approached Sap. Head in advance of line held by B Coy and tried to bomb our party, but were driven off. Trench mortars then became very active and there was also some shelling. Our casualties 1 O.R. killed and 4 wounded.	
Sept 29th.	A Coy relieved C Coy and B relieved D in front line. Except for some trench mortars the day and night were quiet.	
Sept. 30th.	Improvements to trenches continued. Trench mortars active at intervals during day and night and some shelling. Casualty 1 OR wounded.	

7. Pretty Major
4th Suffolk Regt

Army Form C. 2118.

WAR DIARY
or
INTELLIGENCE SUMMARY.
(Erase heading not required.)

1/4th Bn Suffolk Regt.

Hour, Date, Place	Summary of Events and Information	Remarks and references to Appendices
Sept 1/16	The Battalion left camp near DERNANCOURT at 3 pm, and proceeded by motor busses to ALLONVILLE, arriving at 5 pm. Went into billets for the night	
Sept 2nd	Marched at 10.30 pm to CANDAS, arriving at 5.35 am, and went into billets.	
Sept 3rd	Church Parade at 9.30 am. Lt E.H. ENRAGHT, 2nd Lts. F.H. WOODCOCK, H. BRANDON, and E. HIGNETT joined the Battalion. Lieut. A.E. FOERSTER R.A.M.C. also reported for duty as M.O.	
Sept 4th	Left CANDAS at 12.30 pm and marched to REMAISNIL arriving at 3.45 pm and went into billets	
Sept 5th	Left REMAISNIL at 11.0 am and marched to BOUBERS-SUR-CANCHE, arriving 2.25 pm.	
Sept 6th	Left BOUBERS-SUR-CANCHE at 9.30 am, and marched to MONTS-EN-TERNOIS arriving 12.40 pm. A & B Coys billeted there, and C Coy at BUNEVILLE.	T. Betty Major 4 Suffolk Regt.

Army Form C. 2118.

WAR DIARY
or
INTELLIGENCE SUMMARY.
(Erase heading not required.)

1/4th Bn Suffolk Regt.

Hour, Date, Place	Summary of Events and Information	Remarks and references to Appendices
Sept. 7th.	Day was spent in Coy Inspections, and cleaning kit	
Sept. 8th.	Left MONTS-EN-TERNOIS at 8.30 a.m. and marched to WARLUZEL, arriving at 12.15 p.m., and went into billets.	
Sept. 9th.	Parades under Coy Officers.	
Sept. 10th (Sunday)	Church Parade at 9.30 am. C.O. inspected all companies during afternoon.	
Sept. 11th.	Left WARLUZEL at 4.30 am and marched to GAUDIEMPRÉ, arriving 9.40 a.m. A Coy went into billets in the village and the remainder into canvas shelters S.E of it.	
Sept. 12th.	Training proceeded with. Draft of 100 O.R. joined Bttn. D Coy moved into billets in the village.	F. Pretty Major 1/4 Suffolk Regt

WAR DIARY
or
INTELLIGENCE SUMMARY.
(Erase heading not required.)

Army Form C. 2118.

4th Suffolk Regt.

Hour, Date, Place	Summary of Events and Information	Remarks and references to Appendices
Sept. 13th	Training proceeded with.	
Sept. 14th	Training proceeded with.	
Sept. 15th	Training proceeded with. Weather turned colder	
Sept. 16th	The Battalion had the use of the Divl baths at GUADIEMPRÉ, and training proceeded as usual.	
Sept. 17th	Church Parade at 10.0 a.m. Lieut Col H.C. Copeman D.S.O. was awarded the Order of St Stanislaus 3rd class. Draft of 100 men joined the Battalion.	
Sept. 18th	Very wet. Capt H Pretty and 2/Lt A.W. Woods rejoined the battalion.	7. Pretty. Major 4th Suffolk Regt.
Sept. 19th	Officers visited SAILLY-AU-BOIS and reconnoitred approaches to HEBUTERNE.	

WAR DIARY
or
INTELLIGENCE SUMMARY.
(Erase heading not required.)

Army Form C. 2118.

1/4th Bn Suffolk Regt.

Hour, Date, Place	Summary of Events and Information	Remarks and references to Appendices
Sept. 20th.	Regt. Gouxtembrig at 4.30 pm and marched to SAILLY-AU-BOIS, where we relieved the 1st Middlesex Regt. We arrived at SAILLY at 6.20 pm and relief was complete at 7.45. Regt. then became reserve Regt. to right of right Bn. Sub Section. Furnished working party of 3 officers and 120 O.R at 9.30 pm and another of 3 Officers and 120 O.R at 3.30 am.	
Sept 21st.	Washing out and well. Chief day of improving billets. Furnished fatigue of 30 men at 9.30 am and 3.30 pm.	
Sept 22nd.	Improved billets. Furnished working parties of 240 men at various times during day and night.	
Sept 23rd.	Improved billets and furnished working parties of 86 men at various times of day and night.	
Sept 24th.	Billets improved, and working parties of 360 men furnished at various times.	

F. Preston
Major
4th Suffolk Regt.

98th Brigade.

33rd Division.

1/4th BATTALION

THE SUFFOLK REGIMENT

OCTOBER 1916

VOL 13

Army Form C. 2118.

WAR DIARY
or
INTELLIGENCE SUMMARY.   1/4 Bn Suffolk Regt
(Erase heading not required.)

Hour, Date, Place	Summary of Events and Information	Remarks and references to Appendices
Oct 1st 1916.	Work on improving trenches continued.	
" 2nd "	Weather turned very wet. The Regt was relieved by the 1/8 Royal Warwicks, relief being completed by 5.30 pm. Companies marched independently to St ARMAND, and billeted for the night.	
" 3rd "	Fell in at 9.30 am and marched to SUS-ST-LEGER and went into billets. Weather very wet.	
" 4th "	Wet weather interfered with training. Officers attended lecture by G.O.C. D Division, and tactical exercise by G.O.C. Bde in afternoon.	
" 5th "	Company training. C.O inspected the Battalion in the afternoon.	
" 6th "	Training continued.	
" 7th "	Training continued.	

F. Pretor Major
1/4th Suffolk Regt.

Army Form C. 2118.

WAR DIARY
or
INTELLIGENCE SUMMARY.
(Erase heading not required.)

1/4th Bn Suffolk Regt.

Hour, Date, Place	Summary of Events and Information	Remarks and references to Appendices
Oct 8/16	C.O. and Company Officers reconnoitred line. Very wet weather.	
" 9 "	Company continued training. Lecture by G.O.C. Division for Senior officers.	
" 10 "	Training continued in morning. Inspection by Maj. Gen. R.J. Pinney during afternoon.	
" 11 "	Very wet weather.	
" 12 "	Training continued.	
" 13 "	Training continued.	
" 14 "	Company training during morning, and a half holiday in afternoon.	
" 15 "	Bn Church Parade in morning, with short drill parade afterwards.	

F. Roth Major
1/4 Suffolk Regt.

1/4th Suffolk Regt.

Army Form C. 2118.

WAR DIARY
or
INTELLIGENCE SUMMARY.
(Erase heading not required.)

Instructions regarding War Diaries and Intelligence Summaries are contained in F.S. Regs., Part II. and the Staff Manual respectively. Title pages will be prepared in manuscript.

Hour, Date, Place	Summary of Events and Information	Remarks and references to Appendices
Oct. 16 SUS-ST.LEGER.	Quiet morning with the Brigade under Brigadier General Maitland C in G D.S.O, in the morning. C.O and Coy Officers attended lecture on "Tanks" at LUCHEUX in the afternoon.	
Oct. 17th		
" 18th	Training continued.	
" 19th	Received orders to be prepared to move at short notice. Transport left by road for TALMAS at 12.30 pm in the snow. Fell in at 10.45 am, and entrained. Started at 1.15 pm, and after a tedious journey arrived at CORBIE at 4.50 pm. Billeting arrangement completed about 9.45 pm. Transport arrived at 10.25 pm.	
" 20th	Remained in billets at CORBIE.	
" 21st	Paraded at 4.40 am and marched to CAMPAS camp. S.E. of MÉAULTE, arriving 1.25 pm.	

F. Pretty Major
1/4th Suffolk Regt.

Army Form C. 2118.

1/4th Bn Suffolk Regt

WAR DIARY
or
INTELLIGENCE SUMMARY.
(Erase heading not required.)

Instructions regarding War Diaries and Intelligence Summaries are contained in F.S. Regs., Part II. and the Staff Manual respectively. Title pages will be prepared in manuscript.

Hour, Date, Place	Summary of Events and Information	Remarks and references to Appendices
Oct. 22nd	Spent the day in camp. Weather turned cold	
" 23rd	Left MÉAULTE at 9.25 a.m. and marched to BRIQUETERIE, arriving at 1.20 p.m. and occupied bivouacs.	
" 24th	Moved from BRIQUETERIE to TRONES WOOD, starting at 4.0 p.m. Bivouacked in the open. Heavy rain.	
" 25th	Remained at TRONES WOOD. Furnished a working party of 70 men. C and B Coy officers reconnoitred line.	
" 26th	Remained at TRONES WOOD. Furnished working parties of 350 men. Heavy rain.	
" 27th	Remained at TRONES WOOD. Furnished working parties of 325 men. Heavy rain.	
" 28th	Furnished working parties numbering 135 men and relieved the 1/8th Middlesex Regt in DEWDROP TRENCH E of LES BOEUFS. have commenced at 4.20 p.m. and relief was completed at 2.30 a.m. D Coy in the front line. B in support. A + C in reserve.	

J. Prest, Major,
1/4 Suffolk Regt

Army Form C. 2118.

1/4 H.B.r Suffolk Regt

WAR DIARY
or
INTELLIGENCE SUMMARY.
(Erase heading not required.)

Hour, Date, Place	Summary of Events and Information	Remarks and references to Appendices
Oct. 28th Contd.	An attempt was made by D Coy to push forward outposts on to the ridge further East, but it was found to be already occupied by enemy in strength and attempt very severe. Casualties 5. O.R. killed. 9 O.R. wounded.	
Oct. 29th.	At 6.0 p.m. a second attempt was made by D Coy to occupy ridge, but enemy was found in strong position, and attempt failed. B Coy sent 2 Platoon up. Heavy rain. Casualties 2/Lt E. HIGNETT wounded. D Coy advanced the line on to the ridge about 100 yds in front for a length of 400 yds or their left.	
Oct. 30th.	C Coy relieved B Coy in front and support line. Heavily shelled all night. Casualties 4 O.R. killed. 9 O.R. wounded. 3 O.R. missing.	
Oct. 31st.	C Coy attempted but failed to capture the rest of the ridge at 6.0 p.m., and again at 5.30 a.m. On the left our line was	F. Pretty Major 1/4 Bn 1/4 Bn Suffolk Regt

WAR DIARY

INTELLIGENCE SUMMARY

Army Form C. 2118.

1/4 Bn Suffolk Regt.

Hour, Date, Place	Summary of Events and Information	Remarks and references to Appendices
Oct 31st Coled	Explored 100 yds to the right. 2 Platoon of A Coy relieved 2 Platoons of B coy to the front line. Is again very wet. Casualties - 2/Lt E.G. Joyce Killed, 2/Lt C.A. Harris wounded. 5 O.R. killed, 12 O.R. wounded. 1 O.R. missing. C.O received congratulations of Corps Commander on work done since taking over line.	

F. Pretty Major.
1/4th Suffolk Regt.

98th Brigade.
33rd Division.
-----o-----

1/4th BATTALION

THE SUFFOLK REGIMENT

NOVEMBER 1 9 1 6

Army Form C. 2118.

WAR DIARY
of
INTELLIGENCE SUMMARY.
(Erase heading not required.)

4th Batt. Suffolk Regt.

Remarks and references to Appendices.

9 Oct 14

Hour, Date, Place	Summary of Events and Information
November 1st	A party of "A" company under 2nd Lt. G. H. C. Adams attacked the enemy position on ridge on our right front in conjunction with an attack made by Brigade on our right. Our artillery bombardment had not destroyed enemy machine gun which caused us several casualties including 2nd Lt. G. H. C. Adams killed and the party was forced to fall back. Relieved by 1st Middlesex Regt. Relief started at 5:30 and was complete by 8:50 p.m. and regiment proceeded to FLERS LINE. O.R. Casualties {Killed 5 / Wounded 12
November 2nd	Remained in FLERS LINE. Furnished working parties of 150 men. 1 O.R. wounded.
November 3rd	Relieved by 5th Battalion Scottish Rifles at 5:30 p.m. and proceeded to Hutments on MONTAUBAN — CARNOY road.
November 4th	Remained in Hutments
November 5th	Left Hutments at 8.0 a.m. and proceeded to Canvas camp near MEAULTE arriving at 1.5 p.m.
November 6th	Spent day cleaning up.
November 7th	Remained in Camp.
November 8th	Transport left by road 12 noon.

J. Pretty Major
1/4th Suffolk Regt.

Army Form C. 2118.

WAR DIARY
of
INTELLIGENCE SUMMARY.
(Erase heading not required.)

4th Suffolk Regiment

Instructions regarding War Diaries and Intelligence Summaries are contained in F. S. Regs., Part II. and the Staff Manual respectively. Title pages will be prepared in manuscript.

Hour, Date, Place	Summary of Events and Information	Remarks and references to Appendices
November 9th	Battalion moved 10.0.a.m. and marched to EDGEHILL where they entrained and left for LONPRE arriving 4.30 p.m. and then marched "A" "B" companies to CRUMONT, "C" to LIMERCOURT, Headquarters and "D" coy to HUCHENNEVILLE. Arrived very tired about 10.0 p.m.	
November 10th	"C" company moved to CRUMONT and "A" company to HUCHENNEVILLE.	
November 11th	Companies parade for inspections and refitting.	
November 12th	Church Parade 11.0.a.m.	
November 13th	Spent day refitting and cleaning up.	
November 14th	Refitting and cleaning up, proceeded with.	
November 15th	Battalion went for Route March.	
November 16th	Training continued.	
November 17th	Training continued.	
November 18th	Training continued.	

F. Pretty Major
1/4th Suffolk Regt.

WAR DIARY
or
INTELLIGENCE SUMMARY.
(Erase heading not required.)

4th Suffolk Regiment.

Army Form C. 2118.

Hour, Date, Place	Summary of Events and Information	Remarks and references to Appendices
November 19th	Voluntary church service were held.	
November 20th	The Battalion went for short route march. Training continued.	
November 21st	Training continued. The Regiment played 1st Middlesex Regt. at football and lost 4-2.	
November 22nd	Training proceeded.	
November 23rd	Training proceeded.	
November 24th	The Battalion went for route march.	
November 25th	Training continued.	
November 26th	G.O.C. Division Major General Pinney came to Battalion headquarters and presented the Military Medal ribbon to the following N.C.Os. and men:— 2899. Sgt. A.E. Everson. 6574. Cpl. A. Capon. 1501. Sgt. J. Trotter. 2390. Cpl. L. Smith. 1703. Sgt. J. Dodd. 3217. L/Cpl. E. Shepherd. 1863. Sgt. G. Simpson. 3509. Pte. O. Marten. 2193. L/Sgt. C.A. Pizzey.	F. Pretty Major 1/4th Suffolk Regt.

Army Form C. 2118.

WAR DIARY
or
~~INTELLIGENCE SUMMARY.~~ 4th Suffolk Regt.

(Erase heading not required.)

Instructions regarding War Diaries and Intelligence Summaries are contained in F. S. Regs., Part II. and the Staff Manual respectively. Title pages will be prepared in manuscript.

Hour, Date, Place	Summary of Events and Information	Remarks and references to Appendices
November 27th	Training continued.	
" 28th	Training continued.	
" 29th	Training continued.	
" 30th	Training continued.	

F. Pretty Major
1/4th Suffolk Regt

98th Brigade.

33rd Division.

1/4th BATTALION

THE SUFFOLK REGIMENT

DECEMBER 1 9 1 6

98th Brigade.

33rd Division.

1/4th BATTALION

THE SUFFOLK REGIMENT

DECEMBER 1 9 1 6

WAR DIARY
or
INTELLIGENCE SUMMARY.
(Erase heading not required.)

Army Form C. 2118.

1/4 Bn Suffolk Regt

Vol 15

Hour, Date, Place	Summary of Events and Information	Remarks and references to Appendices
December 1st 1916 HUCHENNEVILLE	Training continued	
" 2nd	Training continued. Capt S. Scrimgeour joined the Bn for duty	
" 3rd	Reorganisation. Church Parade in morning.	
" 4th	Transport moved to ARGOEUVES. by road.	
" 5th	Transport moved by road to BRAY-SUR-SOMME. Remainder of Bn entrained at PONT REMY & proceeded to MERICOURT, where they marched to BRAY-SUR-SOMME arriving about 9 p.m. Billets were very bad.	
BRAY-SUR-SOMME " 6th	C.O. & Coy Commanders visited the lines during the day.	
" 7th	Remained at BRAY-SUR-SOMME	
" 8th MARICOURT	Bn moved to Camp 107 near BILLON WOOD (MARICOURT) went very smoothly	

R. Cheverin Lt Col
Commdg 4 Suff R.

Army Form C. 2118.

WAR DIARY
or
INTELLIGENCE SUMMARY.
(Erase heading not required.)

1/4th Bn Suffolk Regt.

Instructions regarding War Diaries and Intelligence Summaries are contained in F.S. Regs., Part II. and the Staff Manual respectively. Title pages will be prepared in manuscript.

Hour, Date, Place	Summary of Events and Information	Remarks and references to Appendices
December 9th, 1916 MAUREPAS	C.O. & Bn Commrs visited the lines in the morning. Bn moved off at 2.15 pm to Maurepas Camp arriving	
10-	about 4.30 pm Capt S. EASTON R.A.M.C. joined the Bn for duty as M.O. Bn relieved 2 companies of the 19th Chesnires & half a 2 companies of the 26th Bavarians in front trench of the 25th French Infantry Bde in trenches N.E. of BOUCHAVESNES.	
TRENCHES		
11-	A & C Coys relieved the 19th Chesnires commanded by Capt VILLAEM, in the front line. D Coy was in support & B Coy in reserve. Casualties 1 O.R. killed Trenches very bad. Relief completed by 9.45 p.m.	
LE FOREST 12-	Bn was relieved by 16 K.R.R.C. & marched into Bde Reserve near LE FOREST (at PETIT BOIS) arriving about 3 a.m. Casualties 1 O.R. killed, 1 wounded Remained at PETIT BOIS.	
13-	Remained at PETIT BOIS.	
TRENCHES 14-	Relieved 4 Kings in trenches N.E. of BOUCHAVESNES. A & C Coys front line, D in support, B in reserve. Relief completed 10.30 p.m. Casualties 1 O.R. wounded.	Lt Corgan Able Bourne Ashe

(73989) W4141—463. 400,000. 9/14. H.&J.Ltd. Forms/C. 2118/10.

WAR DIARY
INTELLIGENCE SUMMARY.
(Erase heading not required.)

Army Form C. 2118.

1/4 Bn Suffolk Regt.

Hour, Date, Place	Summary of Events and Information	Remarks and references to Appendices
December 15th 1916 TRENCHES	Much the same in form & character. Enemy quiet. Improvements to trenches continued. 'B' & 'D' relieved 'A' Coy & 'D' Coy. 'C' Coy. Casualties 2 O.R. wounded.	
" "	Improvements to trenches continued. Station quiet except for occasional moments of shelling. Casualties 1 O.R. wounded. Bn was relieved by 9 H.L.I & moved back in the 19 Bt let to MARICOURT & thence by bus to Bray & then	
SUZANNE	near SUZANNE arriving the about 7 a.m. in the 9 Bt Casualties 1 O.R. wounded. During the time of tour at the Bristol End of the line was in the hundred in the Division.	
" "	Cleaning up clothes & equipment.	
" "	Cleaning up clothes & equipment.	
" "	Improvement carried on during the morning. L/C Hammond 1/4 B/d awarded D.C.M. with Major Gen'l Pinney G.O.C. 33 Dn. Commanding 1/4 S.R.	

Lt Col B.N. Simpkin

WAR DIARY
INTELLIGENCE SUMMARY

Army Form C. 2118.

1/4th Bn Suffolk Regt.

Hour, Date, Place	Summary of Events and Information	Remarks and references to Appendices
December 22nd 1916 MAUREPAS	Bn marched at 11.30 a.m. to camp near MAUREPAS where they arrived at 1.30 p.m. in Bde Reserve.	
23rd	A few shells from heavy guns fell near camp but did not do any damage. C.O. & 2 Coy Commanders reconnoitred L.O. on the front held by 4 Kings in trenches S.W. of RANCOURT.	
24th	Bn relieved the 4 Kings in trenches S.W. of RANCOURT. Casualties 1 killed 3 wounded. Relief complete 9.30 p.m. Trenches extremely muddy & wet & it was impossible to get up to the front line at all at night. Rations & water had to be brought up - Russian prisoners were employed on this during the night.	
25th TRENCHES	Enemy aeroplane came over B in afternoon.	1/2 Cpl Spencer RFA. Wounded 4 Suff R.

WAR DIARY
INTELLIGENCE SUMMARY

Army Form C. 2118.

1/4th Bn S. Staff. Regt.

Hour, Date, Place	Summary of Events and Information	Remarks and references to Appendices
December 26th 9 a.m.	Much aerial activity — enemy aeroplanes flying very low over our lines dropping bombs. Heavy rifle fire etc. Bombardment still of little consequence. Relieved by 1/5th S.W.B. of 119th I. Bde at 11 p.m. Marched to camp 111 near shower bath & from there by lorry to Camp 30 near BRAY-SUR-SOMME arriving about 3 a.m. Between RANCOURT and MAUREPAS we had to march in platoons owing to shell fire.	Bn. H.Q. C company 4 Staff. Regts.
BRAY-SUR-SOMME 8 p.m.	Personnel in camp cleaning up generally.	

WAR DIARY
or
INTELLIGENCE SUMMARY.
(Erase heading not required.)

Army Form C. 2118.

1/4th Bn Suffolk Regt.

Hour, Date, Place	Summary of Events and Information	Remarks and references to Appendices
December 29/1916	Transport moved by road to ARGOEUVES. Remainder of Bn marched to EDGEHILL STA. near DERNANCOURT, proceeded by train to LONGPRÉ, & marched thence to VILLERS-SOUS-AILLY arriving about 3 a.m.	
VILLERS-SOUS-AILLY " 30th	Transport rejoined the Bn about 4.30 p.m.	
" 31st	General cleaning up.	

J. Garnons H.C.C.
Comm'g 4 Suff. Regt.

WAR DIARY
or
INTELLIGENCE SUMMARY.
(Erase heading not required.)

1/4 Suffolk Regt Vol 16

Army Form C. 2118.

Hour, Date, Place	Summary of Events and Information	Remarks and references to Appendices
1917		
Jan 1st VILLERS bois AILLY	Training commenced.	
Jan 2nd	Arrival of draft of 68 men. Training continued	
Jan 3rd	"	
Jan 4th	"	
Jan 5th	"	
Jan 6th	The Bn had Xmas dinners during the afternoon by Companies. The Divisional Band played for an hour and a half in the Square.	

Lt Colonel ?

WAR DIARY
or
INTELLIGENCE SUMMARY.
(Erase heading not required.)

Army Form C. 2118.

Hour, Date, Place	Summary of Events and Information	Remarks and references to Appendices
Jan 7th VILLERS sous AILLY	Voluntary Church Service.	
Jan 8th " "	Three Officers joined the Bn Lt J.G. BROWN 2/Lt B.C. RIGBY 2/Lt A.W.HARE	
Jan 9th	Football match v 1st Middlesex at BRUCAMPS. Result:- 1st Middlesex 4 goals 4th Suffolks 1 "	
Jan 10th	Bn Route March through MOUFLERS and BOUCHON	
Jan 11th	The Bn competed in a Bde Cross-country run Inphlping 24 competitors. Result:- 1st Middlesex 1st 2nd F&SH 2nd 4th King's 3rd 4th Suffolks 4th	
Jan 12th	Sgt V.S. GREY came in first for the Bn.	[signature]

(73989) W4141—463. 400,000. 9/14. H.&J.Ltd. Forms/C. 2118/10.

WAR DIARY
or
INTELLIGENCE SUMMARY.
(Erase heading not required.)

Army Form C. 2118.

Instructions regarding War Diaries and Intelligence Summaries are contained in F.S. Regs., Part II. and the Staff Manual respectively. Title pages will be prepared in manuscript.

Hour, Date, Place	Summary of Events and Information	Remarks and references to Appendices
Jan 11th VILLERS and AILLY	Training continued.	
Jan 12th	Training continued	
Jan 13th	Bn Parade followed by practice of an attack from trenches.	
Jan 14th	Church Parade in the morning. The Senior Chaplain of the Division took the service after which the F.O.C. Division presented the military medal to Pte G.A. Whiting.	
Jan 15th	Training continued.	
Jan 16th	The G.O.C. Bde inspected all the recent drafts which amounted to about 200 men. 2Lt F. Dallimer and 2nd A.L.C. Games joined the Bn.	
Jan 17th	Bn route march via MOUFFLERS and BOUCHON. Billeting party start to Camp 12.	J.R. Grosvenor Lt Col

Army Form C. 2118.

WAR DIARY
or
INTELLIGENCE SUMMARY.
(Erase heading not required.)

Instructions regarding War Diaries and Intelligence Summaries are contained in F.S. Regs., Part II and the Staff Manual respectively. Title pages will be prepared in manuscript.

Hour, Date, Place		Summary of Events and Information	Remarks and references to Appendices
Jan 18th	VILLERS-sous-AILLY	Transport start to Camp 12 via ABBEVILLE	
Jan 19		Bn start to Camp 12 at 5.15am marching to LONGPRÉ in the snow and going by train to ERSINEUL. The Bn arrived at Camp 12 about 2/3 m, a very bad camp with one hundred in the huts or beds.	
Jan 20	Camp 12	B. march to Camp 18 via BRAY and BÉCORDEL, a much better camp than Camp 12	
Jan 21	Camp 18	Bn relieve the French Bn Relief in HOWITZER WOOD being complete about 9.30 p.m.	
Jan 22	HOWITZER WOOD	Remain at HOWITZER WOOD	
Jan 23	HOWITZER WOOD	Bn relieve the 1st R. Warwick in the front line just South of BOUCHAVESNES	
Jan 24	TRENCHES	Remain.	

(73989) W4141—463. 400,000. 9/14. H.&J.Ltd. Forms/C. 2118/10.

WAR DIARY
or
INTELLIGENCE SUMMARY.
(Erase heading not required.)

Army Form C. 2118.

Instructions regarding War Diaries and Intelligence Summaries are contained in F.S. Regs., Part II. and the Staff Manual respectively. Title pages will be prepared in manuscript.

Hour, Date, Place	Summary of Events and Information	Remarks and references to Appendices
Jan 25th TRENCHES	The enemy surprised A Coy right listening post from the rear after an artillery barrage taking 5 prisoners at about 5.30 am. In the evening "B" and "C" Coys relieved "A" and "C" Coys in the front line.	
Jan 26th	B Coy sent out a patrol in white coats which examined the enemy wire and searched for enemy listening posts with the object of surprising one. The enemy however had no posts beyond his wire which was too thick to be penetrated without artillery preparation.	
Jan 27th "	The Bn was relieved by the 9th H.L.I. and proceeded to camp near SUZANNE arriving about 4 am Jan 28th.	
Jan 28th	Remain in camp.	

WAR DIARY
or
INTELLIGENCE SUMMARY.
(*Erase heading not required.*)

Army Form C. 2118.

Hour, Date, Place	Summary of Events and Information	Remarks and references to Appendices
Jan 29th Camp 19	Fitting of gum boots and bathing at SUZANNE	
Jan 30th "	As for Jan 29th	
Jan 31st "	G.O.C. XV Corps inspected camp in the morning. Bn left camp at 5 pm to relieve 5th Scottish Rifles in support of night sector in CLERY SUR SOMME.	

Vol 7
Army Form C. 2118.

1/4th Bn Suffolk Regt

WAR DIARY
or
INTELLIGENCE SUMMARY.
(Erase heading not required.)

Hour, Date, Place	Summary of Events and Information	Remarks and references to Appendices
Feb. 1st Trenches.	Furnished working parties numbering 2 Offrs & 120 O.R.	
Feb. 2nd "	O.C and Company officers reconnoitred front line. Furnished working parties numbering 50 men	
Feb. 3rd "	Relieved the 2nd A & S Hrs in front line (Right Sector of Right Brigade) Relief commenced at 6.30 p.m and was completed at 9.15 p.m. 'A', 'B', and 'C' Coys in front line; 'D' in reserve.	
Feb. 4th "	Except for rifle grenades and small trench mortars, our line was quiet. 1. O.R killed.	
Feb. 5th "	Enemy rifle grenade active. Lieut. J. Gordon Brown killed and 3. O.R wounded.	Fretton Major 1/4th Suffolk Regt.

Army Form C. 2118.

WAR DIARY
or
INTELLIGENCE SUMMARY
(Erase heading not required.)

1/4th Bn Suffolk Regt.

Hour, Date, Place	Summary of Events and Information	Remarks and references to Appendices
Feb. 6th Trenches	"D" Coy relieved "A" Coy on left of the line. 1 O.R. killed and 1 O.R. wounded.	
Feb. 7th "	Some shelling and grenades 2 O.R. wounded.	
Feb. 8th "	"B" Coy took over right of line and "C" Coy the centre.	
Feb. 9th "	Relieved by 4th Bn King's Liverpool Regt. Relief commenced 6 pm and was complete by 8 pm. We moved into reserve support.	
Feb. 10th "	Furnished working parties numbering 2 Offs & 140 OR. Remainder of men rested.	
Feb. 11th "	Furnished working parties numbering 3 Offs & 180 OR. Casualties — 1 OR killed and 3 OR wounded.	F. Preston Major 1/4th Suffolk Regt.

Army Form C. 2118.

WAR DIARY
or
INTELLIGENCE SUMMARY.
(Erase heading not required.)

1/4th Bn Suffolk Regt.

Hour, Date, Place	Summary of Events and Information	Remarks and references to Appendices
Feb. 12th Trenches.	Relieved 4th Kings in front line. 'A' 'B' and 'D' Coys in front line and 'C' in reserve. Relief commenced 5-30 pm and finished at 8 pm.	
Feb. 13th Trenches.	At 9.30 pm we raided the German trenches with a party consisting of 2/Lieut's L.P. BENNETT and A.W. HARE, and 53 other ranks. Casualties were inflicted on the enemy. Our casualties were:- 2/Lt. L.P. BENNETT badly wounded, 1 OR killed, 3 OR missing believed killed, 5 OR wounded. Official report attached	
Feb. 14. Trenches.	'C' Coy relieved 'B' in front line.	
Feb. 15. "	Information received that 2/Lt. L.P. BENNETT had died of wounds at No 5. C.C.S. on 14/2/17.	F. Pretty, Major 1/4th Bn Suffolk Regt.

Army Form C. 2118.

WAR DIARY
INTELLIGENCE SUMMARY.
(Erase heading not required.)

1/4th Suffolk Regt.

Hour, Date, Place	Summary of Events and Information	Remarks and references to Appendices
Feb. 16. Trenches.	Enemy artillery and trench mortars active very. The Batt.n was relieved by the 2nd Norfolk Regt. Relief commenced at 6.30pm and was finished at 10.30pm. The Regt. marched to Camp 19, SUZANNE, reaching there at 3-30am.	
Feb. 17. Camp 19.	Spent day cleaning up.	
Feb. 18. "	Cleaning up continued.	
Feb. 19. "	Batt.n spent day having baths, drawing, fitting and testing new Small box respirators, and fitting gum boots and clothing.	
Feb. 20th "	Company training in adverse weather. Extra attention being given to bombers and Lewis gunners.	F. Foster Major 1/4th Suffolk Regt.

Army Form C. 2118.

WAR DIARY
or
INTELLIGENCE SUMMARY
(Erase heading not required.)

1/4th Bn Suffolk Regt.

Hour, Date, Place	Summary of Events and Information	Remarks and references to Appendices
Feb. 21st Camp. 19.	Company training continued.	
Feb. 22nd — " —	Company training	
Feb. 23rd — " —	Company training	
Feb. 24th — " —	Company training.	
Feb. 25th — " —	The Battalion moved into Reserve at HOWITZER WOOD and relieved the 6th Scottish Rifles. Left Camp 19 at 4.15pm and completed relief by 5.30 pm	
Feb. 26th HOWITZER WOOD	Relieved the 4th King's Liverpool Regt. in the line in the Right & Left Section. Platoons from HOWITZER WOOD at 5.30 am. Relief was completed by 12.15 am (27th) without casualties. 'A' Coy on the Right, 'B' Centre, 'C' in Support, and 'D' on Left.	F. Pretty Major 1/4th Suffolk Regt.

Army Form C. 2118.

WAR DIARY
INTELLIGENCE SUMMARY

1/4th Bn Suffolk Regt.

(Erase heading not required.)

Hour, Date, Place	Summary of Events and Information	Remarks and references to Appendices
Feb.27 Trenches	Quiet day except for trench mortars.	
Feb.28 "	During the early morning heavy trench mortars landed in trenches occupied by D Coy on left, one killing 6 OR and another killing 1 OR and wounding 1 OR. Relieved by 4th King's Liverpool Regt. Relief started at 4.45 pm and was completed by 11.45 pm. Casualties 7 OR killed & 4 OR wounded. We moved to support line ROAD WOOD	

J. Pretty Major
1/4th Suffolk Regt.

REPORT ON RAID CARRIED OUT BY THE 1/4th SUFFOLK REGIMENT
AT 9.30 P.M., FEBRUARY 13th, 1917.

At Zero the parties who had been formed up in our trench by the sap got out and lay down in front of our wire, in the order in which they were to go over. They followed up the barrage, lead by 2/Lieut. L.P.Bennett, and as it lifted the first party got through the German wire, and entered the trench at about I.7.d.08.65. 2/Lieut. Bennett established his Headquarters at this point, and the first party pushed down the trench to the right (South), under Sergt. T.Lamb. Before they had gone far they discovered a dug-out; they shouted to the occupants to come up and they did so, the first having an overcoat over his head. The party pushed on for at least another 40 yards, meeting little or no opposition, and did not find anything. The prisoners were sent back under an escort of 2 men to 2/Lieut.L.P.Bennett, who sent them under the same escort back to our line. On reaching the enemy wire, a shell or mortar, (believed to have been one of our own) fell amongst them and killed them all. (Their remains can be seen in the enemy wire this morning). Time now about 9.45 p.m. In the meantime the second party had entered the enemy trench directly after the first, and had moved North. Before going far, however, they encountered a strong party of the enemy; these parties bombed each other, and progress became very slow.

The third party got into the trench behind the second party, and, owing to the second party making slow progress, found themselves very crowded.

2/Lieut. A.W.Hare, who was leading this party, pushed forward to discover what had happened to the second party. He succeeded in reaching a small latrine, from which he was able to throw bombs. He considers that altogether the second party must have inflicted considerable casualties on the enemy party, but they were only able to make very slow progress up the trench, one reason for this being that the leading bayonet man of the second party had become a casualty.

The enemy were throwing the majority of their bombs over the heads of the second party into the third party, who were crowded, but the throwing was bad and we sustained few casualties. 2/Lieut.L.P.Bennett, who was controlling the three parties with great coolness, ordered the third party to ease back a little as they were crowded. (Time about 9.48 p.m.)

Shortly after this 2/Lieut.L.P.Bennett was badly wounded in the thigh. This left the parties without a leader, and just then the bugle was blown at the prearranged time. This was unfortunate, as the second party had not had time to make much progress Northwards, owing to the opposition they encountered.

We sustained a few casualties as our men returned to our trench from fragments of shell and mortar.

The strength of the raiding party was 2 Officers and 58 Other Ranks.
Our total casualties amounted to:-
1 Officer wounded severely.
1 Other Rank killed.
3 Other Ranks missing (believed killed).
5 Other Ranks wounded.

The Medium T.M. Officer told me yesterday that he had not been able to register before the raid.

(sd)H.C.Copeman, Lieut.Col.,
Commdg. 1/4th Suffolk Regiment...

14/2/17.

Army Form C. 2118.

War Diary № 1/B
1/4th Bn Suffolk Regt.

WAR DIARY
INTELLIGENCE SUMMARY
(Erase heading not required.)

Hour, Date, Place	Summary of Events and Information	Remarks and references to Appendices
April 1st ROAD WOOD	Remained at ROAD WOOD in support. 2 OR wounded.	
March 2nd "	Relieved the 4th King's Liverpool Regt. in left of left Sector. Relief commenced at 4.30 pm and was completed by 11.30. "A" Coy right, "B" centre, "C" left, "D" in support.	
March 3rd TRENCHES.	Quiet day. Worked on improving trenches. Very little hostile activity.	
April 4th "	Demon. on our left delivered an attack, and a smoke cloud and rockets were put up from our trench which drew some hostile artillery fire which did very little damage. Relieved by 4th King's Liverpool Regt. in the evening. Relief started 4.30 pm and was completed by 10.30. We then went into support at HOWITZER WOOD reaching there about 12.15 am. Casualties 1 OR killed 6 OR wounded.	G. Cummins? Capt. 1/4 Suffolk ?

Army Form C. 2118.

WAR DIARY
INTELLIGENCE SUMMARY.
(Erase heading not required.)

14th Suffolk Regt.

Hour, Date, Place	Summary of Events and Information	Remarks and references to Appendices
April 5th HOWITZER WOOD.	Remained in reserve at HOWITZER WOOD. Had 4 inches of snow during the night.	
April 6th SUZANNE	Arrived at tent camp at SUZANNE leaving at 10am and getting in at 1.30pm.	
April 7th SUZANNE and SAILLY LAURETTE.	Left SUZANNE at 10am and marched to Camp 184 near SAILLY LAURETTE arriving at 1.30pm. Weather very cold.	
April 8th SAILLY LAURETTE. hard 9th "	Spent day cleaning up & refitting. New clothing issued etc. Major Gen. R.J. PINNEY, C.B. addressed the Battalion. Weather very cold.	
April 10th "	Company training.	
April 11th "	Voluntary Services.	

Lt. Commanding 14th Suffolk Regt.

WAR DIARY
INTELLIGENCE SUMMARY

Army Form C. 2118.

1/4th Bn Suffolk

Hour, Date, Place	Summary of Events and Information	Remarks and references to Appendices
Mar. 12 Camp 12↑	Company Training	
" 13 "	Route march in morning and training continued. 2/Lt. H.R. WOLTON joined the Bn	
" 14 "	Company Training	
" 15 "	Route march and field training	
" 16 "	Baths at SAILLY-LAURETTE at the disposal of the Battalion. Company Training. The Regtl Transport was inspected by Brig. Genl. G.D.T. Maitland, C in C. D.S.O.	
" 17 "	Route marches and field training. 2/Lt S.W. TURNER joined the Bn	
" 18 "	Voluntary Services.	1/c. Greenwell Left 6 nd. 1st Suffolks Bn.

WAR DIARY or **INTELLIGENCE SUMMARY.**

Army Form C. 2118.

1/4 Suffolk Regt

Hour, Date, Place	Summary of Events and Information	Remarks and references to Appendices
Apr 19. Campo 1917	Training continued. Cpl 1798 Sgt W. JERMYN was awarded the Italian Bronze Medal for Military Valour.	
" 20 "	Revr'l March and Company training. 2/Lt C.C.S. GIBBS was appointed Adjutant of the Battalion and is to be gzt. (Lieut) whilst so employed. Appointment to be dated 1-1-1917. Draft of 2 O/R joined the Bn.	
" 21 "	Training continued.	
" 22 "	Route marches and training.	
" 23 "	Training continued.	

Lt Colonel H.F.L.
Cmd 1/4 Suffolk Regt

Army Form C. 2118.

WAR DIARY
or
INTELLIGENCE SUMMARY.
(Erase heading not required.)

1/4th Bn. Suffolk Regt.

Hour, Date, Place	Summary of Events and Information	Remarks and references to Appendices
March 24th Camp 124	Training Continued. Route approach. Blankets were disinfected.	
March 25 Camp 124	Voluntary services in Church Army Hut. Newly joined men fitted in new box respirators.	
March 26th Camp 124	Training Continued	
March 27th Camp 124	Training Continued. Capt. Hon. M.G. Tollemache joined the Bn for duty and was posted to 'A' Coy.	
March 28th Camp 124	Two companies practised attacking a position in the open. Gas Demonstration in the afternoon for C.O. & Coys and the M.O. Capt. Hon. M.G. Tollemache assumed command of 'D' Coy. Capt G. O.B. Bennison proceeded to VILLERS BRETONNEUX & to be attached for one month to the A.D.O.S. III Corps	Lr. Whyman Lieut Col. Comndg 1/4th Suffolk Regt

Army Form C. 2118.

WAR DIARY
INTELLIGENCE SUMMARY.
(Erase heading not required.)

1/4 Bn. Suffolk Regt.

Hour, Date, Place	Summary of Events and Information	Remarks and references to Appendices
March 29 Camp 124	Bn Route March to MOREAUCOURT, marching past General RJ Pinney CB & Div who in his speech took the Leather Jerkins handed in... afterwards of the Bn	
March 30 Camp 124	Two days practised attacking a position in the open.	
March 31 Camp 124	The Bn practised attacking a position in the open. Preparations for move made	

In. Copeman Lieut Col
Commanding 1/4 Suffolk Regt

Army Form C. 2118.

Vol 1/7
1/4th Bn Suffolk Reg.t

WAR DIARY
or
INTELLIGENCE SUMMARY.
(Erase heading not required.)

Instructions regarding War Diaries and Intelligence Summaries are contained in F.S. Regs., Part II. and the Staff Manual respectively. Title pages will be prepared in manuscript.

Hour, Date, Place	Summary of Events and Information	Remarks and references to Appendices
April 1st Camp 124.	Bn moved at 9.45 A.M. & marched to LA NEUVILLE les CORBIE arriving 12 noon & going into billets.	
April 2nd LA NEUVILLE.	Moved at 12.15 P.M & marched to MOLLIENS AU BOIS arriving 4.5 P.M & going into billets. Very heavy snow storm during latter part of the march.	
April 3rd MOLLIENS-au-BOIS	Moved at 1 P.M & marched to NAOURS arriving 4.30 P.M & going into billets. Weather very cold.	
April 4th NAOURS.	Moved at 8.5 A.M & marched to LONGUEVILLETTE arriving 12.10 P.M & going into billets. Snow during first part of march. 2nd Lieut V.S. GREY joined the battalion.	
April 5th LONGUEVILLETTE	Moved at 11.35 A.M & marched to BEAUREPAIRE FARM arriving 3.10 P.M. Billeted in the farm. Here we came into the 3rd Army area & joined the XVIII Corps.	

(73989) W4141—463. 400,000. 9/14. H.&J.Ltd. Forms/C. 2118/10.

WAR DIARY
or
INTELLIGENCE SUMMARY.
(Erase heading not required.)

Army Form C. 2118.

1/4th T. Sutton Regt

Hour, Date, Place	Summary of Events and Information	Remarks and references to Appendices
April 6th BEAURETAIRE.	Remained here & spent the day in church parades & inspections. Very wet afternoon.	
April 7th BEAURETAIRE.	Moved at 8.20 A.M. & marched to COUIN arriving 12.15 P.M. & were accommodated in a hut camp.	
April 8th COUIN	Moved at 11.15 A.M. & marched to BERLES-au-BOIS arriving 2 P.M. & going into billets G.O. & Bt. Cy. McCarthy & remainder in Coysul Valley	
April 9th BERLES-au-BOIS.	We were now on 3 hour notice to move. The day was spent in final inspection & all surplus kit dumped.	
April 10th BERLES-au-BOIS	The day was taken up with Coy; parades.	
April 11th BERLES-au-BOIS.	Received orders to move & marched at 7 P.M., our destination being the BLAIRVILLE-FICHEUX area. The weather was bitterly cold & it snowed heavily. About 11 P.M. we halted for the night & breakfast MADELAIN REDOUBT near to where the railway crosses the FICHEUX-MERCATEL Rd.	

Army Form C. 2118.

WAR DIARY
or
INTELLIGENCE SUMMARY.
(Erase heading not required.)

1/4th Suffolk Regt

Hour, Date, Place	Summary of Events and Information	Remarks and references to Appendices
April 12th MADELAIN REDOUBT.	Received orders to relieve the 18th Manchester Regt in close support at N.26.C.0.9 on the NEUVILLE-VITASSE–HENIN-SUR-COJEUL Rd. Leaving the redoubt at 1.5. P.M the relief was complete by 5.40 P.M. A chance shell fell amongst "C" Coy on the way up killing 1 & wounding 3 O.R. 1st reinforcements & "B" Echelon of the Regt remained at BLAIRVILLE. Casualties 1.O.R Killed 3 O.R wounded including one return 16 in and 1st Regt	
April 13th N.26.C.0.9	A great deal of burial & salvage work was done by the battalion in the vicinity of the trenches in front of the high ground Casualties 4 O.R wounded	
April 14th N.26.C.0.9	Bn remained in close support & continued the burial & salvage work. 1st reinforcements & "B" Echelon move to BOISLEUX-au-MONT	
April 15th N.26.C.0.9	Salvage work continued. Casualty 1 O.R wounded	

Army Form C. 2118.

WAR DIARY
or
INTELLIGENCE SUMMARY.
(Erase heading not required.)

1/4th Suffolk Regt

Instructions regarding War Diaries and Intelligence Summaries are contained in F.S. Regs., Part II and the Staff Manual respectively. Title pages will be prepared in manuscript.

Hour, Date, Place	Summary of Events and Information	Remarks and references to Appendices
April 16th N.26.c.0.9.	Relieved the 1st Cameronians in the right sub-sector of the front line which included the Hindenburg line & one Coy: front to the N.O.K. Relief was much delayed & not completed till next morning. Enemy shelled Tuelos busy heavy group.	
April 17th Trenches.	Relief of 1st Cameronians finished at 9.30 a.m. & we took over the line with C.A.B.D. on right, centre, left & support respectively. Casualties 4. O.R. Killed 13 O.R. wounded	
April 18th Trenches.	A lot of work was done joining gaps between Coys in front line.	
April 19th Trenches.	Improvement & construction of trenches continued. Casualties 1. O.R. wounded	

Army Form C. 2118.

WAR DIARY
or
INTELLIGENCE SUMMARY.
(Erase heading not required.)

1/4th Suffolk Regt

Hour, Date, Place	Summary of Events and Information	Remarks and references to Appendices
April 20th Trenches	Relieved by the 20th Royal Fusiliers, relief being completed by 5.30 P.M. The Regt returned to its previous position at N.2.b. Casualties 6. O.R. wounded.	
April 21st N.2.b.	Day spent cleaning up. Casualties 1. O.R. killed 1. O.R. wounded	
April 22nd N.2.b.	Moved up & relieved 20th Royal Fusiliers, starting 2.25 P.M. relief was complete by 4.30 P.M. Disposition of Coy C.A.B. D. Right, centre, left & support respectively. Casualties 1. O.R. killed 2. O.R. wounded.	

(73889) W4141—463. 400,000. 9/14. H.&J.Ltd. Forms/C. 2118/10.

Army Form C. 2118.

WAR DIARY
or
INTELLIGENCE SUMMARY.
(Erase heading not required.)

1/4th Suffolk Regt.

Hour, Date, Place	Summary of Events and Information	Remarks and references to Appendices
April 23rd Trenches.	The battalion took part in a general assault on the German position, their objective being the front & support trenches of the Hindenburg line as far as the SENSÉE RIVER, a distance of about 2,300 yards. "C" Coy supported by "D" were to work down the front line on the right & "A" supported by "B" down the support line on left. The following officers went into action with the battalion. Head Qrs. Lt Col. H.C. COPEMAN D.S.O. Commanding. Lieut C.C.S. GIBBS adjt.; Capt J. GASTON (R.A.M.C) M.O. "A" Coy. Capt H. PRETTY, 2nd Lieuts F. DALLIMER, B.S. EVANS "B" Coy. Capt T.J.C. RASH, 2nd Lieuts A.W. HARE, D. GLEN, B.C. RIGBY, "C" Coy. 2nd Lieut C.S. GOFF, W.R. WOLTON, F. ADAMS, H.W. WOODS, "D" Coy. Lieut H. HOYLAND, E.H. ENRAGHT, H.G. TOPHAM, 2.G.O. 2nd Lieut S.C. WILLIAMS. Sig: Officer 2nd Lieut F.H. WOODCOCK. After artillery preparation the advance commenced at 4.45 A.M. "A" & "B" Coy worked up the support trench meeting with a good deal of opposition of all sorts until reaching	1st Command HQ 1/4 6/7th Regt

Army Form C. 2118.

WAR DIARY
or
INTELLIGENCE SUMMARY.

(Erase heading not required.)

1/4th Suffolk Regt

Place	Date	Hour	Summary of Events and Information	Remarks and references to Appendices
(Continued)	April 28th		the second sunken road about 200 yards short of their objective at 6.30 A.M. Here they were met with trenchmortars, rifle & M.G. fire & held up. They maintained themselves there till 9 A.M. when the enemy counter-attacked strongly, & being much in advance of the troops on both flanks, were compelled to withdraw to their original starting point or be cut off. "C" & "D" Coys advancing up the front line trench with the assistance of one Tank also met with considerable opposition but reached the sunken road about 9.30 A.M. & remained till 2 P.M. when the counter attacks & the enemy in the trench behind made it necessary to quit the trench & return over the open to the south, re-entering the French in rear of their original barricade. They rejoined Bn at 5.30 P.M. During the night we were relieved by the 1st Cameronians & when morning broke out of the trenches next morning learnt that the enemy had retired & the ground occupied by us the day before had been occupied. In the course of the action we captured about 650 unwounded prisoners five machine guns & one trench-mortar. Our casualties were	

J.G. Garnier Lt Col
1/4 Suffolk Regt

Army Form C. 2118.

WAR DIARY
or
INTELLIGENCE SUMMARY.
(Erase heading not required.)

1/4th Suffolk Regt.

Place	Date	Hour	Summary of Events and Information	Remarks and references to Appendices
	April 24th		(continued) Killed 2nd Lieut H.W. WOODS & 41. O.R. Wounded. Capt J.C. RASH, 2nd Lieuts. W.R. WOLTON, A.W. HARE, T. DALLIMER, D. GLEN, B.C. RIGBY, B.S. EVANS, S.C. WILLIAMS & 160. O.R. Missing. 104. O.R.	
BOYELLES. BIVOUAC.	April 25th		Relief by the 1st Cameronians completed by 8.30 A.M. & we proceeded to bivouac in the vicinity of BOYELLES arriving there at 1.P.M. M.O. & a party returned to scene of action found & buried the body of 2nd Lieut WOODS & brought in 2nd Lieut HARE & 11 wounded men. Moved at 1.30 P.M. & marched to BRETENCOURT arriving 4.30 P.M. & going into billets. Inspected afterwards by BLAIRVILLE by Corps Commander.	
BRETENCOURT	April 26th		Day spent refitting. 2nd Lieut W.G. HAINES & 118 O.R. joined the battalion	

Army Form C. 2118.

WAR DIARY
or
INTELLIGENCE SUMMARY.
(Erase heading not required.)

1/4th Suffolk Regt

Place	Date	Hour	Summary of Events and Information	Remarks and references to Appendices
BRETENCOURT	April 27th		Day spent refitting & re-organising coys & platoons	
BRETENCOURT.	April 28th		Bath marched to the battalion. Capt T.S. CUBITT 5.O.R. joined the	
BRETENCOURT	April 29th		Brigade church parade under Brigadier General J.D. HERIOT-MAITLAND, C.M.G, D.S.O. Commanding 98th Infy Bde. Officers & 200 O.R. from the battalion attended. Lieut-General Sir T.D'O. SNOW K.C.B, K.C.M.G commanding VII Corps & Major-General R.J. PINNEY, C.B commanding 33rd Division were also present. At the conclusion of the service the Corps Commander addressed the Bde & presented a large number of medals to NCOs & men of the 2nd Bn Argyll & Sutherland Highlanders & 1st Bn Middlesex Regt	

(A7092). Wt. W14859/M1293. 750,0.0. 1/17. D. D. & L., Ltd. Forms/C.2118/14.

Army Form C. 2118.

WAR DIARY
or
INTELLIGENCE SUMMARY.
(Erase heading not required.)

1/4th Suffolk Regt

Instructions regarding War Diaries and Intelligence Summaries are contained in F.S. Regs, Part II. and the Staff Manual respectively. Title pages will be prepared in manuscript.

Place	Date	Hour	Summary of Events and Information	Remarks and references to Appendices
BRETENCOURT	April 30th		Brigadier General J.D. HERIOT-MAITLAND C.M.G. D.S.O. addressed the Officers & N.C.O's of the battalion & expressed his satisfaction with the manner in which the task of attacking the Hindenburg trenches had been carried out by them. Parade under company arrangements.	J. Spencer Maj 1/4 Suffolk Regt 30/4/17

Army Form C. 2118.

WAR DIARY
or
INTELLIGENCE SUMMARY.
(Erase heading not required.)

1/4th Suffolk Regt.

Vol 20

Instructions regarding War Diaries and Intelligence Summaries are contained in F. S. Regs., Part II. and the Staff Manual respectively. Title pages will be prepared in manuscript.

Place	Date	Hour	Summary of Events and Information	Remarks and references to Appendices
BRETENCOURT	May 1st		Baths & Coy parades in morning. In the afternoon C.O. Officers & N.C.O.'s attended a brigade conference & shown the action of April 23rd. Major-General R.J. PINNEY C.B. was also present. The following officers joined the battalion. 2nd Lieuts:- J. C. Cooper, S.L. Goulding, W.P. Fisher, G.W. Fincher, L.C. Palmer R.A. Hayward, S.H.C. Waller. Also 149 O.R.	
BRETENCOURT	May 2nd		Moved at 1.15 P.M. & marched to DOUCHY LES AYETTE arriving 4.5 P.M., & bivouaced.	
DOUCHY	May 3rd		Issue of new clothing. Coy parades.	

Lt. Cyr ... L.R.
4th Suffolk Regt

Army Form C. 2118.

WAR DIARY
or
INTELLIGENCE SUMMARY.
(Erase heading not required)

1/4th Suffolk Regt

Place	Date	Hour	Summary of Events and Information	Remarks and references to Appendices
May 4th DOUCHY			Parades 7.15–7.45 A.M. & 9.15 A.M. to 12.30 P.M, with platoon conferences & Tactical exercise under C.O. in afternoon 2.6.O.R joined the battalion	
May 5th DOUCHY			Parades 7.15–7.45 A.M & 9.15 A.M to 12.30 P.M. Platoon conferences & a tactical exercise under C.O. in afternoon	
May 6th DOUCHY			Church Parade at 11 A.M A mounted gymkhana under brigade arrangements was held in the afternoon. It was largely attended & much enjoyed by all ranks. There were six events, of which two namely the relay race for Company Commanders Horses & the relay race for pack-ponies were won by this regt.	

In. Corpenau Lt. Col.
1/4 Suffolk Regt

Army Form C. 2118.

WAR DIARY
or
INTELLIGENCE SUMMARY.   1/4TH SUFFOLK REGT

(Erase heading not required.)

Instructions regarding War Diaries and Intelligence Summaries are contained in F. S. Regs., Part II. and the Staff Manual respectively. Title pages will be prepared in manuscript.

Place	Date	Hour	Summary of Events and Information	Remarks and references to Appendices
DOUCHY	MAY 7TH		Bathn + Coy training in morning. In the afternoon there was a half-holiday + a large number of officers & O.R attended a race-meeting organized by the 33rd Div: The weather was fine & a most enjoyable afternoon was spent	
DOUCHY	MAY 8TH		Heavy rain during the night & forenoon interfered with out-door training. A draft of 55 O.R joined the battalion	
DOUCHY	MAY 9TH		Weather cleared & training proceeded as usual	
DOUCHY	MAY 10TH		Left DOUCHY at 11 A.M & marched to BOYELLES arriving 1.35 P.M & bivouacked in a field S of the village.	
BOYELLES	MAY 11TH		Company parades & camp improved	

In Command
1/4 Suffolk Regt

Army Form C. 2118.

WAR DIARY
or
INTELLIGENCE SUMMARY.

(Erase heading not required.)

1/4th SUFFOLK Regt

Instructions regarding War Diaries and Intelligence Summaries are contained in F.S. Regs., Part II. and the Staff Manual respectively. Title pages will be prepared in manuscript.

Place	Date	Hour	Summary of Events and Information	Remarks and references to Appendices
BOYELLES	MAY 12TH		Company training.	
BOYELLES	MAY 13TH		Church parade at 11 A.M.	
BOYELLES	MAY 14TH		Company training. C.O. & officers reconnoitred the line	
BOYELLES	MAY 15TH		Relieved the 2nd A. & S. Highlanders in the right sub-sector of the line. The relief was complete by 10.15 P.M. with "B" Coy supported by "A" on the right & "D" Coy supported by "C" on the left. Reinforcement & "B" echelon remained at BOYELLES.	
TRENCHES	MAY 16TH		Routine work of trenches. Carrying parties from support companies & "B" echelon were furnished for work up the HINDENBURG TRENCH.	
TRENCHES	MAY 17TH		Trenches. Carrying parties furnished. Casualty. 1. O.R. Killed	
TRENCHES	MAY 18TH		Trenches. Carrying parties furnished	

J.V. Grimwade Lt Col
1/4 Suffolk Regt

Army Form C. 2118.

WAR DIARY
or
INTELLIGENCE SUMMARY.
(Erase heading not required.)

1/4TH SUFFOLK REGT

Instructions regarding War Diaries and Intelligence Summaries are contained in F. S. Regs., Part II and the Staff Manual respectively. Title pages will be prepared in manuscript.

Place	Date	Hour	Summary of Events and Information	Remarks and references to Appendices
TRENCHES	MAY 19TH		Trenches. Carrying parties furnished. Casualty 1 O.R. Wounded	
TRENCHES	MAY 20TH		33rd Division attacked the German position with a view to capturing the FONTAINE-CROISILLES-HENDECOURT ROAD. The first attack was launched at 5.15 A/M & was partially successful & was renewed again at 7.30 P.M. when further progress was made. The regiment were not called upon to leave the trenches during these operations & at the conclusion of the day we became battalion in brigade support. Casualties 1 O.R. Killed, 2 O.R. Wounded	
TRENCHES	MAY 21ST		It was thought that the brigade would be required to push on down the HINDENBURG LINE, the regiment was detailed for this work & preparations made accordingly. At 12 noon however the arrangements were cancelled & we remained in brigade support. The line was heavily shelled throughout the day. Casualty 1 O.R. wounded	
TRENCHES	MAY 22nd		Weather turned very wet.	

[signature] Lt. Commanding
1/4 Suffolk Regt

Army Form C. 2118.

WAR DIARY
or
INTELLIGENCE SUMMARY.
(Erase heading not required.)

1/4th SUFFOLK REGT

Instructions regarding War Diaries and Intelligence Summaries are contained in F. S. Regs., Part II. and the Staff Manual respectively. Title pages will be prepared in manuscript.

Place	Date	Hour	Summary of Events and Information	Remarks and references to Appendices
TRENCHES	MAY 23rd		Relieved the 2nd Bn A. & S. H. & one company 1st Middlesex Regt in the right sub-sector relief was completed at 11.30. P.M. & 3 A.M. respectively. The names of the following officers appeared in the gazette as mentioned in dispatches. Lt Colonel Capeman D.S.O.; Capt B L. J. Richards & J. C. Rash also Sergt Major J. S. Newman & Sergt C. Barker	
TRENCHES	MAY 24th		Several patrols were sent out. There was considerable shelling of the line especially in the evening. Casualties 2 O.R. killed & 1 O.R. wounded	
TRENCHES	MAY 25th		The battalion was relieved from the 4th King's Liverpool Regt & proceeded to bivouacs in the vicinity of BOYELLES, getting back about 2.30 A.M. Capt E. L. D. LAKE; Lieut H. K. STADDON; 2nd Lieuts R. FISHER & W. P. WESTWOOD & 61 O.R. joined the Bn.	
BOYELLES	MAY 26th		Day spent resting, cleaning up & improving bivouacs	

Army Form C. 2118.

WAR DIARY
or
INTELLIGENCE SUMMARY.
(Erase heading not required.)

1/4th SUFFOLK REGT

Instructions regarding War Diaries and Intelligence Summaries are contained in F.S. Regs., Part II. and the Staff Manual respectively. Title pages will be prepared in manuscript.

Place	Date	Hour	Summary of Events and Information	Remarks and references to Appendices
BOYELLES	MAY 27th		Church parade at 9 A.M. at which Major-General R.J. Pinney C.B., Brigadier-General J.D. Herist-Maitland C.M.G., D.S.O. were present, at the conclusion of the service the former presented decorations to the following officers N.C.O.s + men. Military Cross. Capt. J. Gaston (R.A.M.C.); Lieut. + Adjt C.C.S. Gibbs. Military Medal. Sergt G.W. Spice & A.C. Roper; L/Cpl B.C. Smith & B. Lincoln; Private A.W. Parker, J.H. Chaplin, T.H. Sommerford, R.C. Markham, A. Lilley. The following awards were also made but the recipients owing to wounds or sickness were unable to be present Military Cross. 2nd Lieut. B.S. Evans & W.R. Wolton. Distinguished Conduct Medal. Corpl S.P. Blake. Military Medal. Sergt J. Albon, Corpl A. Larkin, L/Cpl W. Butt & N. Wilson, Privates H. Leek, W.R. Emmerson, V.G. Borley. At the conclusion of the presentations the Divisional General complemented Lt Colonel Copeman & the regiment on the part it had played in the action of April 23rd.	Sgd. Copeman Lt Col 1/4 Suff Rgt

Army Form C. 2118.

WAR DIARY
or
INTELLIGENCE SUMMARY.
(Erase heading not required)

1/4th SUFFOLK REGT

Place	Date	Hour	Summary of Events and Information	Remarks and references to Appendices
BOYELLES	MAY 28TH		Relieved 4th Kings Liverpool Regt in trenches taking over sector of HINDENBURG LINE. Relief was completed 2 A.M. "D" on right, "A" on left, "B" right support, "C" left support. Nothing to the number of men + isolated posts to be occupied. It was a difficult relief.	
TRENCHES	MAY 29TH		Deepened + improved trenches + reorganised + numbered various posts. Casualties 3 O.R. wounded.	
TRENCHES	MAY 30TH		Connected some of the posts + put out 200 yards of wire. There was a thunderstorm some rain. Casualties 1 O.R. killed + 2 O.R. wounded. 2/Sergt F. BOAST was awarded the Medaille Militaire	
	MAY 31ST		Relieved by 9th Bn K.O.Y.L.I. + proceeded to camp at HENDECOURT LEZ RANSART where the regiment arrived by 3.15 A.M. During the day trenches were heavily shelled + much knocked about. During the relief there was considerable hostile shelling with gas shells. We were extremely fortunate however + casualties not in proportion to the weight of metal dropped being only 1 O.R. killed + 6 O.R. wounded	

Sd. Crownest Lt Col
1/4 Suffolk Regt

Army Form C. 2118.

WAR DIARY
or
INTELLIGENCE SUMMARY.
(Erase heading not required.)

1/4th SUFFOLK REGT

Instructions regarding War Diaries and Intelligence Summaries are contained in F. S. Regs., Part II. and the Staff Manual respectively. Title pages will be prepared in manuscript.

Place	Date	Hour	Summary of Events and Information	Remarks and references to Appendices
HENDECOURT	JUNE 1st		Regiment was into camp by 3.15 A.M. This day was fine & spent resting & improving camp. Whole above company inspection	JP
HENDECOURT	JUNE 2nd		Company drill for one hour in the morning, afternoon clothing inspection.	JP
HENDECOURT	JUNE 3rd		Church parade at 11 A.M. 2nd Lieuts C.G. Sykes & E.M. Pullen & 18.O.R. joined	JP
HENDECOURT	JUNE 4th		Company training from 9 A.M. to 12.45 P.M. In the afternoon one company on rifle range, remainder bathing, football etc.	JP
HENDECOURT	JUNE 5th		Company training from 9 A.M. to 12.45 P.M. In the afternoon one company on rifle range, remainder bathing, football etc.	JP
HENDECOURT	JUNE 6th		Company training in morning. Rifle range in use by one Coy in afternoon.	JP
HENDECOURT	JUNE 7th		Company training in morning. Inspection by Corps Commander Lt. General Sir T. D'O. Snow K.C.B; K.C.M.G in the afternoon.	JP

Army Form C. 2118.

WAR DIARY
or
INTELLIGENCE SUMMARY.
(Erase heading not required.)

1/4th SUFFOLK REGT

Instructions regarding War Diaries and Intelligence Summaries are contained in F. S. Regs., Part II. and the Staff Manual respectively. Title pages will be prepared in manuscript.

Place	Date	Hour	Summary of Events and Information	Remarks and references to Appendices
HENDECOURT	JUNE 8th		Company training in morning. Rifle shooting, football in afternoon	
HENDECOURT	JUNE 9th		Company training in morning. Rifle shooting + various games in afternoon.	
HENDECOURT	JUNE 10th		Church Parade 9.30 A.M. A letter from the East Suffolk County Council to the Commanding Officer was read after the service. The letter conveyed the Council's congratulations to all ranks + expressed their appreciation of the service rendered by the regiment in the field.	
HENDECOURT	JUNE 11th		Wet weather interfered with out-door training.	
HENDECOURT	June 12th		Company training in morning. The preliminary heats for the athletics sports were run off in the afternoon + concert under battalion arrangements were held from 6 to 8 P.M.	

Army Form C. 2118.

WAR DIARY
or
INTELLIGENCE SUMMARY.
(Erase heading not required.)

1/4th SUFFOLK REGT

Instructions regarding War Diaries and Intelligence Summaries are contained in F. S. Regs., Part II. and the Staff Manual respectively. Title pages will be prepared in manuscript.

Place	Date	Hour	Summary of Events and Information	Remarks and references to Appendices
HENDECOURT	June 13th		Company training proceeded as usual till 11.30 A.M. From 2 to 7 P.M. athletic sports were held. Fifteen events with good entries in all were competed for. The weather was perfect & the divisional band played selections during the afternoon.	
HENDECOURT	June 14th		Company training proceeded.	
HENDECOURT	June 15th		Short parades in morning. In afternoon field-firing practice on range at RANSART	
HENDECOURT	June 16th		Company training in morning. Rifle [exercises] & games in afternoon	
HENDECOURT	June 17th		Church parade at 9.45 A.M.	

[signature] Lt Col.

WAR DIARY
or
INTELLIGENCE SUMMARY.

(Erase heading not required.)

Army Form C. 2118.

1/4th SUFFOLK REGT

Place	Date	Hour	Summary of Events and Information	Remarks and references to Appendices
HENDECOURT	JUNE 18TH		Short parade in morning. Field firing in RANSART range in afternoon. The 305 Qui concert party "The Shrapnels" gave an excellent entertainment from 6.30 to 8 P.M.	AP
HENDECOURT	JUNE 19TH		Wet morning somewhat interfered with out-door work. Inter-company foot-ball league matches were concluded in the afternoon. Results: "D" Coy first, "C" Coy second. In the evening from 6 to 8 P.M. a battalion concert was held & much appreciated.	AP
HENDECOURT	JUNE 20TH		In the morning a field firing competition for prizes presented by the C.O. for the best section of 8 men under an N.C.O was shot for, resulting in a win for "B" Coy with "A" Coy second. Remainder of the day spent in cleaning up the camp & preparing to move which we did at 5 P.M, marching to bivouac E. of BOYELLES relieving the 10th Bn K.O.Y.L.I. & becoming battalion in reserve to left brigade. Relief complete by 7.25 P.M.	AP

M. Grammell Lt Col

Army Form C. 2118.

WAR DIARY
or
INTELLIGENCE SUMMARY.
(Erase heading not required.)

1/4th SUFFOLK REGT

Place	Date	Hour	Summary of Events and Information	Remarks and references to Appendices
BOYELLES	JUNE 21st		Short parade for inspection & remainder of day put in work constructing camp	
BOYELLES	JUNE 22nd		Company parades & much work on camp improvement	
BOYELLES	JUNE 23rd		Company parades & work on camp. C.O. & officers reconnoitred the line.	
BOYELLES	JUNE 24th		Church parade 9.45 A.M. Relieved the 2nd Bn A.&S.H. taking over the left of the Divisional sector in the HINDENBURG LINE (SHAFT TRENCH) from FOP LANE to the SENSEE RIVER. Relief was complete by 6.15 P.M. 'A' Coy on right + 'B' Coy left in front line, 'D' Coy support + 'C' Coy reserve.	
TRENCHES	JUNE 25th		Worked on improvement to trenches a day fairly quiet	

Army Form C. 2118.

WAR DIARY
or
INTELLIGENCE SUMMARY.
(Erase heading not required.)

1/4th SUFFOLK REGT.

Place	Date	Hour	Summary of Events and Information	Remarks and references to Appendices
TRENCHES	JUNE 26TH		Worked on trenches, quiet day but towards evening enemy commenced shelling. During the night all available men worked to dig a new trench eastward along RIVER ROAD. 170 yds were completed to a depth of 3 ft. Hostile shelling uneventful towards dawn.	
TRENCHES	JUNE 27TH		As soon as it was light, enemy noticed the new trench & commenced to shell it heavily & continued to do so which it was practically obliterated the posts holding it had to be withdrawn. During the day the front & support lines were also heavily shelled & trenches very much knocked about. 'D' 'B' 'A' & 'C' in front in. 1st Lieut H.G. HAYNES + 2 O.R. killed + 2 O.R. Wounded. Casualties.	
	JUNE 28TH		Work repairing damaged trenches carried out. A good deal of hostile shelling during morning & night. Then remain comparatively quiet. Supplied A & C sect. of infantry. Casualties 4 O.R. wounded.	
	JUNE 29TH		At 8.50 A.M. hingate on our left delivered a small attack. Our trenches were again shelled. Casualties 2 O.R. wounded. Capt H.D. MITCHELL 2nd Lieut E.W. GARLAND + H.B. HUTCHERSON + 67 O.R. joined the battalion.	

W. Crossman L/C

Army Form C. 2118.

WAR DIARY
or
INTELLIGENCE SUMMARY.

(Erase heading not required.)

1/4th SUFFOLK REGT

Place	Date	Hour	Summary of Events and Information	Remarks and references to Appendices
TRENCHES.	JUNE 30th		Weather turned wet. Relieved by 10th YORKSHIRE REGT relief complete by 4.45 P.M. On completion companies comps marched to BOYELLES & entrained on decauville railway & proceeded to BEAUMETZ, detrained & marched to BASSEUX where all were accommodated in billets by 10 P.M. Casualties 1 O.R. killed 1 O.R. wounded.	JB

J.C. Copeman Capt
Comd. 1/4th Suffk. Th. Regt.

WAR DIARY
or
INTELLIGENCE SUMMARY.
(Erase heading not required.)

1/4th Suffolk Regt

Army Form C. 2118.

Vol 22

Place	Date	Hour	Summary of Events and Information	Remarks and references to Appendices
BASSEUX	JULY 1st		Company inspections & cleaning up.	F.P.
BASSEUX	JULY 2nd		Route march of about seven miles in morning. Afternoon spent cleaning up billets preparatory to moving.	F.P.
BASSEUX	JULY 3rd		Left BASSEUX at 5 A.M. & marched via LACAUCHIE, HENU & AUTHIE to ACHEUX where we arrived at 1.5 P.M. & were accommodated in huts. A halt of 1 hr. 10 mts was made for breakfast. The distance about 17 miles. The day very hot tiring & the march very tiring.	F.P.
ACHEUX	JULY 4th	3.40 A.M	Left ACHEUX at 3.40 A.M in pouring rain & marched via RAINCHEVAL, PUCHEVILLERS to TALMAS about 11 miles arriving wet through at 8.35 P.M. & going into billets. Fine afternoon.	F.P.
TALMAS	JULY 5th	4.30 A.M	Left TALMAS at 4.30 A.M. & marched via NAOURS & VIGNACOURT to LACHAUSSÉE a distance of about 13 miles, arriving 9.20+ going into billets. Fine day.	F.P.
LACHAUSSÉE	JULY 6th	4 A.M	Left LACHAUSSÉE 4 A.M. & marched via CROUY, SOUES, LE QUESNOY to WARLUS a distance of about 12 miles arriving 8.35 A.M. The weather was perfect	F.P.

J.R. Chevassue Lt Col
1/4 Suffolk Regt

Army Form C. 2118.

WAR DIARY
or
INTELLIGENCE SUMMARY.
(Erase heading not required.)

1/4th SUFFOLK REGT

Instructions regarding War Diaries and Intelligence Summaries are contained in F. S. Regs., Part II. and the Staff Manual respectively. Title pages will be prepared in manuscript.

Place	Date	Hour	Summary of Events and Information	Remarks and references to Appendices
WARLUS	JULY 7TH		Coy inspections, marking of deficiencies etc. Then rather a footrace after the four days marching. Billets at WARLUS pretty good + weather perfect. 16.D.I.R joined the battalion	F.P.
WARLUS	JULY 8TH	11.20.A.M.	Church parade	F.P.
WARLUS	JULY 9TH		Parades from 8 A.M to 12.30.P.M. In afternoon Divisional band played selection in the square. 4. O.R joined the battalion	F.P.
WARLUS	JULY 10TH		Parades from 8.15.A.M to 12.45 P.M for training	F.P.
WARLUS	JULY 11TH	8.15A.M to 11.45 P.M	Training from 8.15A.M to 11.45 P.M. Major-General R.C. PINNEY C.B. Commanding 33rd Division visited companies whilst at work	F.P.
WARLUS	JULY 12TH		Training proceeded in morning; 2 coy's route march of about 8 miles. The battalion cricket team played the 98th Brigade H.Q. a match in the afternoon. Breaching in a room for Brigade are 98th Brigade H.9164, 4th Suffks.131.	F.P.

Lt. Gowerth R.M.
1/4 Suffolk R.M.

Army Form C. 2118.

WAR DIARY
or
INTELLIGENCE SUMMARY.
(Erase heading not required.)

1/4th SUFFOLK REGT

Instructions regarding War Diaries and Intelligence Summaries are contained in F. S. Regs., Part II. and the Staff Manual respectively. Title pages will be prepared in manuscript.

Place	Date	Hour	Summary of Events and Information	Remarks and references to Appendices
WARLUS	JULY 13TH		Company training in morning. Football & other games in afternoon.	T.P.
WARLUS	JULY 14TH		Company training in morning. 2 companies did route march of about 8 miles. Football etc in afternoon. Battalion concert from 6 to 8 P.M. 33 O.R. joined the battalion.	T.P.
WARLUS	JULY 15TH		Church parade at 11.30. a.m. Football etc in afternoon.	T.P.
WARLUS	JULY 16TH		Bn drill under C.O for above, after which there were a gas demonstration by divisional gas-officer. Football in afternoon.	T.P.
WARLUS	JULY 17TH		Company training in morning. Football etc in afternoon. First day of 33rd Divisional Horse Show. Some 70 O.R. went over in lorries. 5 O.R joined the battalion.	T.P.
WARLUS	JULY 18TH		Second day of 33rd Divisional Horse Show. Companies marched independently to the show ground & spent a very enjoyable day.	T.P.
WARLUS	JULY 19TH		Company training in morning. Football etc in afternoon.	T.P.

[signature]
1/4 Suffolk Regt

Army Form C. 2118.

WAR DIARY
or
INTELLIGENCE SUMMARY.

1/4 Suffolk Regt

(Erase heading not required.)

Place	Date	Hour	Summary of Events and Information	Remarks and references to Appendices
WARLUS	July 20th		Company training in morning. Football etc in afternoon. 2nd Lieut H.C. HATTAM + 30 O.R. joined the battalion.	T.P.
WARLUS	July 21st		Company training in morning. Boxing contests in afternoon. 2nd Lieut F.H. CHAINEY joined the battalion	T.P.
WARLUS	July 22nd		Church parade 11.15.	T.Q.
WARLUS	July 23rd		Route march in morning	T.P.
WARLUS	July 24th		Company training + battalion drill in morning. Semi-finals of platoon football competition in afternoon. No 2 platoon beat No 5 platoon by 4 to 1 & No 3 beat No 8 by 4 to nil. Shooting match against 1st An A. & S. Highldrs resulting in a win for the 4th Suffk Regt	T.P.
WARLUS	July 25th		Company training in morning. A marching competition took place between a selected platoon from each company & was won by No 1 platoon of "A" Coy. 3. O.R. joined the battalion	T.P.

Army Form C. 2118.

WAR DIARY
or
INTELLIGENCE SUMMARY.   1/4th SUFFOLK REGT

(Erase heading not required.)

Instructions regarding War Diaries and Intelligence Summaries are contained in F. S. Regs., Part II. and the Staff Manual respectively. Title pages will be prepared in manuscript.

Place	Date	Hour	Summary of Events and Information	Remarks and references to Appendices
	JULY 26TH WARLUS		Company training in morning. Shooting match against 98T.M.B. in afternoon resulting in a win for the battalion.	J.P.
	JULY 27TH WARLUS		Company training in morning. Cricket match against H.Q. 98th Infy Bde resulting in a win for the 98th Bde. Scores 98th Infy Bde 90 4th Suffk Regt 75	J.P.
	JULY 28TH WARLUS		Company training in morning. Final of platoon football matches played in afternoon between Nos 2 & 3 platoons resulted in a draw 2 goals each. Contest was held in the evening from 8 to 9.30 P.M. a successful battalion	J.P.
	JULY 29TH		Heavy rain & thunder-storm during the morning. Church parade 11.50. 2nd Lieuts G.A.W. ALDUS & A.H.H. SYKES joined the battalion. Final of platoon football played off again. No 2 platoon won by 2 goals to nil	J.P.

Lt Col — 4th Suffk Regt

Army Form C. 2118.

WAR DIARY
or
INTELLIGENCE SUMMARY. 1/4th SUFFOLK REGT
(Erase heading not required.)

Instructions regarding War Diaries and Intelligence Summaries are contained in F. S. Regs., Part II and the Staff Manual respectively. Title pages will be prepared in manuscript.

Place	Date	Hour	Summary of Events and Information	Remarks and references to Appendices
WARLUS	JULY 30th		Company training in morning. Afternoon spent in inspections & cleaning up billets preparatory to leaving	F.P
WARLUS	JULY 31st		HdQrs, A, C, & D Coys left WARLUS at 8.30 A.M. & marched to LONGPRÉ arriving at 11.20 A.M. After dinners & teas had been served we entrained & left LONGPRÉ at 6.41 P.M. & travelling throughout the night reached ADINKERKE at 6.5 A.M. 1st Aug/17. B Coy remained at WARLUS. 2nd Lieuts E. CATCHPOLE & W.J.S. COTTON joined the battalion on LONGPRÉ station.	F.P

J.R. Armand Major
1/4th Suffolk Regt

WAR DIARY or INTELLIGENCE SUMMARY

1/5th SUFFOLK REGT

Army Form C. 2118.

Vol 23

Place	Date	Hour	Summary of Events and Information	Remarks and references to Appendices
LA PANNE	Aug 1st		Detrained & left ADINKERKE station at 7.30 A.M. in pouring rain & marched to LA PANNE arriving 8.10 A.M. & going into billets.	F.P.
LA PANNE	Aug 2nd		Company training. Furnished working party of 1 Officer & 50 O.R. for work with Corps heavy artillery	F.P.
LA PANNE	Aug 3rd		Moved billets from the Town to huts on sea-shore & relieved the 1/4th Bn West Riding Regt & took over left sub-section of coast defence extending from FRANCO-BELGIAN FRONTIER to INFANTRY TRENCH. Relief completed at 6 A.M. D Coy furnishing posts & sentries. A coy in support, +B+C in reserve. Very wet day.	F.P.
LA PANNE	Aug 4th		B & C. Coys continued training. A&D improved trenches & post of coast defence.	F.P.
LA PANNE	Aug 5th		Service in Y.M.C.A hut at 9.30 for R.C. Coys. 'A' Coy relieved 'D' Coy in coast defence line & D went into support.	F.P.

B. Greenwell Lt Col

WAR DIARY
or
INTELLIGENCE SUMMARY.

(Erase heading not required.)

1/4th SUFFOLK Regt

Army Form C. 2118.

Instructions regarding War Diaries and Intelligence Summaries are contained in F. S. Regs., Part II. and the Staff Manual respectively. Title pages will be prepared in manuscript.

Place	Date	Hour	Summary of Events and Information	Remarks and references to Appendices
LA PANNE	Aug 6th		B & C Coy training. "A" B. work on coast defence.	T.P.
LA PANNE	Aug 7th		"B" Coy relieved "A" Coy in front + trenches on coast. "C" Coy relieved "D" in support.	T.P.
LA PANNE	Aug 8th		A + D Coy training. Practical demonstration of aeroplane contact work with infantry.	T.P.
LA PANNE	Aug 9th		A. D Coys Training. C Coy relieved B Coy in coast defence line and B went into support. 2nd Lieuts. S.C. ROBERTS and R.S.J. RAMES joined the Regt.	
LA PANNE	Aug 10th		A + D Coys Training. B + C work on coast defence.	

In Grammanffe

Army Form C. 2118.

WAR DIARY
or
INTELLIGENCE SUMMARY.
(Erase heading not required.)

1/4. SUFFOLK REGT.

Instructions regarding War Diaries and Intelligence Summaries are contained in F.S. Regs., Part II. and the Staff Manual respectively. Title pages will be prepared in manuscript.

Place	Date	Hour	Summary of Events and Information	Remarks and references to Appendices
LA PANNE	Aug 11th		D Coy relieved C Coy in Coast Defences and A relieved B in Support	
LA PANNE	Aug 12th		Service in Y.M.C.A. Hut 9.30 am. for A, B, & C Coys.	
LA PANNE	Aug 13th		A Coy relieved D in Coast Defence - D went into Support. B C Coy training. 2nd Lieut. W.L. Evans joined Bn.	
LA PANNE	Aug 14th		B & C Coy Training. A & D work on Coast Defences.	
LA PANNE	Aug 15th		B C Coy Training. Coast Defences taken over by 2nd B" Manchester Regt. Relief complete by 7.0. p.m.	

h Greene Lt Col

Army Form C. 2118.

WAR DIARY
or
INTELLIGENCE SUMMARY. 1/4th Suffolk Regt.
(Erase heading not required.)

Instructions regarding War Diaries and Intelligence Summaries are contained in F. S. Regs. Part II. and the Staff Manual respectively. Title pages will be prepared in manuscript.

Place	Date	Hour	Summary of Events and Information	Remarks and references to Appendices
LA PANNE	Aug. 16th		Batt. left LA PANNE at 6.50 A.M. and marched to Bivouacs at COXYDE, where on arrived at 8.30 a.m. Rest of day was spent in constructing + improving Bivouac Camp. Which was situated at X.13.6.6.8. (Ref map OOST-DUNKERQUE) 1st Reinforcements left Batt. and marched to 33rd Divl. Depot Pt. 19, GHYVELDE.	
COXYDE	Aug. 17th		Morning spent in Inspections, Bathing, etc. (RABAILET) Batt. moved at 3 p.m. to WELLINGTON CAMP (X.5.6.5.5. Map OOST-DUNKERQUE) and relieved (G) 16th NORTHUMBERLAND FUSILIERS in Divisional Reserve. "B" Echelon moved into billets at COXYDE.	
WELLINGTON CAMP	Aug. 18th		Remained at WELLINGTON CAMP.	
"	Aug 19th		Voluntary church service in morning. N.W. end of camp badly shelled with about 8 inch shells; A and C Coys had to bivouac in field South of camp. 6 ORs wounded. Working party of 400 men found in the evening.	
"	Aug 20th		Move to QUEENSLAND CAMP just West of OOST DUNKERQUE which was previously occupied by the 9th H.L.I. A very comfortable and clean camp. Arrived about 8pm.	J.C. Brennan Lt Col

WAR DIARY
or
INTELLIGENCE SUMMARY.
(Erase heading not required.)

Army Form C. 2118.

Place	Date	Hour	Summary of Events and Information	Remarks and references to Appendices
QUEENSLAND CAMP	Aug 21st		Working party of 400 men found as before. The bodies had to be shelled on the return journey. 2Lieut J.W.S. COTTON was wounded in the Thigh and died the following day. 14 ORs were wounded.	
"	Aug 22nd		Remained at QUEEN	
"	Aug 23rd		Bn relieved the 4th King's (L'Pool) Regt in the Rt Subsectors of the pt GEORGES Sector. Relief complete about 2:30am Aug 24th.	
Trenches	Aug 24th		Very little enemy activity. Work done on improving trenches.	
"	Aug 25th		As for Aug 24th. Artillery activity on left at about 10pm.	
"	Aug 26th		Some lights shells fell near Bn HQ between 9.30pm and 10pm. Otherwise quiet.	
"	Aug 27th		Gas shells were projected from our lines at 1am. Arrangements made for relief next day.	

Army Form C. 2118.

WAR DIARY
or
INTELLIGENCE SUMMARY.
(Erase heading not required.)

Place	Date	Hour	Summary of Events and Information	Remarks and references to Appendices
Furnes	Aug 28th		Very strong wind blowing; screens damaged. Bn relieved by 2nd KORLI.	
"	Aug 29th		Relief complete about 2:30am. Move to camp at COXYDE arriving about 5:30am by a bad route. Move to hutt canvas camp at BRAY DUNES arriving at about 4pm.	
BRAY DUNES	Aug 30th		Remained at BRAY DUNES	
	Aug 31st		Transport moved to WORMHOUDT Area and billeting party to EPERLECQUES Area.	

J.C.[signature]

Army Form C. 2118.

WAR DIARY
or
INTELLIGENCE SUMMARY. 1/4th SUFFOLK REGT
(Erase heading not required.)

Vol 24

Place	Date	Hour	Summary of Events and Information	Remarks and references to Appendices
BRAY DUNES.	SEPT. 1ST		Entrained at & left BRAY DUNES 8.55 A.M arriving at WATTEN 12.16 P.M. where we detrained & marched to scattered billets around ZUDROVE & MOULLE getting in about 2.15 P.M. Transport arrived 3.40 P.M. having come by road. No 202129 Pte C. PACKARD was awarded the Military Medal.	T.P.
ZUDROVE.	SEPT 2ND		Church parade 10.30. A.M.	T.P.
ZUDROVE.	Sept 3rd		Coy parades & inspections. Perfect weather.	T.P.
ZUDROVE.	SEPT 4TH		Coy parades & training on Brigade area.	T.P.
ZUDROVE	SEPT 5TH		Coy training for 2 hrs in morning. Marched to rifle range in the afternoon where 64 targets were available from 2.30 to 4.30 P.M. 2 G.O.R. formed station.	T.P.
ZUDROVE.	SEPT 6TH		Coy training in morning. Weather turned wet	T.P.

J.A Grosvenor Lt Col

Army Form C. 2118.

WAR DIARY
or
INTELLIGENCE SUMMARY.

(Erase heading not required.)

1/4th SUFFOLK REGT

Instructions regarding War Diaries and Intelligence Summaries are contained in F. S. Regs., Part II. and the Staff Manual respectively. Title pages will be prepared in manuscript.

Place	Date	Hour	Summary of Events and Information	Remarks and references to Appendices
ZUDROVE	SEPT 7TH		Battalion route march of about 9 miles in morning. The 33rd Divisional concert-party gave two performances during the afternoon + evening which were much appreciated by all ranks. Party of officers reconnoitred forward area. Capt H. Mitchel got wounded.	F.P.
ZUDROVE	SEPT 8TH		Company training in Brigade Area during morning. Played the 4th Kings Liverpool Regt in brigade football league in the afternoon; match resulted in a draw 1 goal each.	F.P.
ZUDROVE	SEPT 9TH		Church parade 10.30 a.m. Played 12th the Middlesex Regt in brigade football league; result we won 2 to nil	F.P.
ZUDROVE	SEPT 10TH		Company training.	F.P.
ZUDROVE	SEPT 11TH		Baths + Company training. Officers reconnoitred forward area. Played the 99th Field Ambulance in brigade football league; result we won 3 goals to nil.	F.P.

N.R. Grooocock Lt Col.

WAR DIARY
or
INTELLIGENCE SUMMARY.
(Erase heading not required.)

Army Form C. 2118.

1/4th SUFFOLK REGT

Place	Date	Hour	Summary of Events and Information	Remarks and references to Appendices
ZUDROVE	SEPT 12TH		Bath + Coy training in morning. Rifle range with 32 targets in afternoon. Played 98th Fd H.Q. in the Brigade football league result we lost 1 to nil	7.P.
ZUDROVE	SEPT 13TH		Battalion training on Brigade area. Concert in the evening from 5.45 - 7.45 P.M.	7.P.
ZUDROVE	SEPT 14TH		Coy training in morning, remainder 1 day spent on inspection & cleaning up before leaving the billets. An aeroplane photograph for Company officers at 2.30 P.M. Section an aeroplane photograph for Brigade football league interclub see lost 1 to nil Played 98th T.M.Bn & M.G.C. in brigade football league	7.P.
ZUDROVE	SEPT 15TH		Moved at 5.30 A.M. + marched to OEHTEZEELE arriving in billets 10.20 A.M.	7.P.
OEHTEZEELE	SEPT 16TH		Moved at 4.30 A.M. + marched via CASSEL to scattered billets about 2½ miles N.E. of STEENVOORDE arriving 10.50 A.M. Voluntary church service 6 P.M.	7.P.

J.R. Garrood Lt. Col.

Army Form C. 2118.

WAR DIARY
or
INTELLIGENCE SUMMARY.
(Erase heading not required.)

1/4th SUFFOLK REGT

Instructions regarding War Diaries and Intelligence Summaries are contained in F.S. Regs., Part II. and the Staff Manual respectively. Title pages will be prepared in manuscript.

Place	Date	Hour	Summary of Events and Information	Remarks and references to Appendices
STEENVOORDE	SEPT 17TH		Marched at 5.30 A.M. via ABEELE & BERTHEN to METEREN getting into billets at 11.40 A.M.	4 P
METEREN	SEPT 18TH		Coy inspection.	
METEREN	SEPT 19TH		Battalion parade 9 A.M. & marched to training area & watched a practice attack by two battalions. Baths in afternoon.	
METEREN	SEPT 20TH		Marched at 4.55 P.M. to the vicinity of RENING HELST where we erected a bivouac camp. Arrived at 10.50 A.M. We now belong to IX Corps.	
RENINGHELST CAMP.	SEPT 21ST		Coy parades & inspection. Played 2nd A.S.H. Hdn in Brigade football league - result we lost 0 – 9 goals	
RENINGHELST CAMP	SEPT 22ND		1st Reinforcement Maj. F. Oakley & officers & 100 O.R. left for division in reserve Bh. Both medical & attested personnel in Bolton area.	

WAR DIARY or INTELLIGENCE SUMMARY

Army Form C. 2118.

Place	Date	Hour	Summary of Events and Information	Remarks and references to Appendices
BELLEGOED FARM	Sept 24		B'n moved forward at 1.15 p.m. & bivouaced near BELLEGOED Farm. Battn up in billets in Bedford House Area.	
	Tuesday Sept 24		Moved up to reserve trenches at CLAPHAM JUNCTION starting at about 7am. 3 Coys to front of Clapham Junction, one at Bee Hut. Remainder of Battn moved up at 1.15pm. Situation until situation reached line being moved up to B'n to attack Hooge Chateau from B Coys S. sharp. Take up position ready for moving forward to the	
	Tuesday Sept 25		Moved at 10.15pm to take up position ready for moving forward to the front line for the attack. Position taken up by 11.30 pm on a line running North from FITZCLARENCE FARM.	
	Tuesday Sept 26		On advance could not be made before 5.45pm owing to Bn on its left not being ready and at about 5.30am the shelling became most intense and heavy casualties were suffered. The heavy shelling, thick midst and darkness caused confusion and it was impossible for the men to keep touch but Platoon rushes were made and some Platoons made progress. Captains Lota and Somagen with about 20 men succeeded in	

N. Spearman Lt Col

Army Form C. 2118.

WAR DIARY
or
INTELLIGENCE SUMMARY.
(Erase heading not required.)

Place	Date	Hour	Summary of Events and Information	Remarks and references to Appendices
Trenches	Sept 27th		reaching the front line and later made a further advance capturing 2 M.G.s and 13 prisoners who gave valuable information. B? began to reform round 23 A.2. B? LONE LANE. Capt Scriven Scriven reported in the forenoon. The relief of the Division commenced in the afternoon and the Bn was ordered to proceed to BEDFORD HOUSE area at 9.15am, it finally arrived in bivouacs at BELGOED Farm at about midnight.	
BELGOED Farm	Sept 28th		For a full account of operations from 7am Sept 24th see attached. The morning was spent cleaning up and collecting stragglers and men who had been detached. At about 4.25pm the Bn moved off to OUDERDOM station and thence by train to EBBLINGHEM. It finally arrived in billets at	
LYNDE	Sept 29th	about 4 A.M.	LYNDE about 4 A.M. (2 Coys remaining at EBBLINGHEM) The Bn remained in billets on 29th resting and cleaning up.	
LYNDE	Sept 30th	9.45am	Church Parade at 9.45am. Remainder of day spent in inspections etc.	

J.V. Grosvenor Lt/Col.
CnO 1/4th Suff to the Rgt

Army Form C. 2118.

WAR DIARY
or
INTELLIGENCE SUMMARY.
(Erase heading not required.)

Place	Date	Hour	Summary of Events and Information	Remarks and references to Appendices
	Sept 30th		The following Casualties occurred during Operations on 25th/26 Sept.	
			2/Lieut. L. C. PALMER. Killed in action.	
			" W. P. WESTWOOD " "	
			Capt. E. L. D. LAKE Wounded	
			A/Capt. S. W. TURNER "	
			" G. G. B. BANNERMAN "	
			2/Lieut. H. C. HATTAM. "	
			" R. FISHER "	
			" S. C. ROBERTS "	
			" R. D. HUME "	
			Other Ranks:—	
			Killed 43 Wounded 150. Missing 68.	

J.R. Grosvenor Major
Cmdg 1/4 Suff. Cy. Regt.

MOVEMENTS OF THE 1/4TH SUFFOLK REGIMENT FROM 24TH TO 28TH SEPTEMBER, 1917.

At 7.0 a.m. on the 24th September the Battalion left the bivouac at BELGOED FARM, moving by ZILLEBEKE track to Headquarters of Brigade on the Eastern edge of SANCTUARY WOOD. There the Battalion halted till 1.0 p.m., the C.O. going forward to examine unoccupied trenches "NEW CUT" and "   ," crossing the YPRES - MENIN Road roughly at right angles in front of CLAPHAM JUNCTION, finding accommodation for barely 3 Companies. These only moved on at 1.0 p.m., and occupied the trenches. Attempts to improve them were followed by shelling - though after events do not show that it was a case of cause and effect - but that shelling was a part of the new offensive of the enemy. The 4th Company remained near Brigade Headquarters. Battalion Headquarters was temporarily in Aid Post at CLAPHAM JUNCTION, as the proper Headquarters were not vacated by the 11th West Yorks Regt. till the evening (C.O. and Adjutant did not leave till 1.0 a.m. 25th). The enemy shelling of the area continued during the night, and increased considerably during the 25th, 2 Company Headquarters being hit (one twice) with 6 fatal casualties.

Due to circumstances in the front line, the previous orders for the 26th attack were changed, and the Battalion, which in the afternoon had sent forward 1 Company to about J.14 central (LONE LANE) to reinforce 2nd A.&.S.Hrs was ordered to take the   originally given to the 1st Middlesex Regt. to attack (from the line to which they had been pressed back in this case) at Zero.

Later, about 7.0 p.m., the C.O. was called to Brigade Headquarters, and received fresh orders to move forward the battalion as soon as possible to a line running along trench from FITZCLARENCE FARM almost North to GLENCORSE WOOD, and to advance with the 5th Scottish Rifles on the Left half of this Front to relieve the Company of 1st Middlesex Regt. and 2nd A.&.S.Hrs on the line running North and South. At first it was thought to be through final 'E' in VERBECK FARM, and later along road in rear of LONE HOUSE.

The 4th Suffolks began moving at 10.15 p.m., and picking up the Company supporting the 2nd A.&.S.Hrs advanced to trench mentioned (North from FITZCLARENCE FARM) which was occupied by 2 Companies, the others in shell holes in rear, by 11.30 p.m.

The C.O. found FITZCLARENCE FARM to be only a concrete strong post of 2 rooms, 1 occupied by F.O.O. and the other by wounded, so unsuited for his Headquarters, so he therefore sent back the personnel of his Headquarters to that of the 2nd A.&.S.Hrs, a strong point at J.14 central. His intentions being to relieve him either as soon as he had placed the Battalion on the forward line, and satisfied himself that it had been properly taken over and all ready for the further move forward, ordered to be made before Zero, so that if possible the actual advance should be made from the original approximate front line at Zero, i.e. roughly BLACK WATCH CORNER - CARLISLE FARM.

The C.O. then proceeded to Headquarters, 1st Middlesex Regt., in a strong post just South of GLENCORSE WOOD, shown thus ∧ on map, J.14.b.3.3. to meet O.C. 5th Scottish Rifles. He was not there, but he met him on his return to the Battalion. He stated that his Battalion was coming up behind him. This would be about 12.0 midnight. Fearful of being late, and as the enemy's intermittent shelling with occasional rifle shots, did not decrease, the C.O. told the C.O. 5th Scottish Rifles

(2)

that he would move forward at 2.0 a.m., but on reference to 98th Brigade this was not allowed. The situation rapidly became worse - the moon was gone, the shelling more regular, and a thick mist rose (or fell). About 3.30 a.m. orders or permission to advance were given if O.C. 4th Suffolks would be responsible for the whole of the 1st Middlesex and 2nd A.&.S.Hrs front. Just then 1¾ Companies of the 5th Scottish Rifles arrived, and shortly after the remainder, some actually coming through from the East of the Line occupied. As it now seemed possible to carry out original orders an attempt was made, but terrible delays occurred, and though first 5.15 a.m. then 5.30 a.m. were fixed by neither hours had the 5th Scottish Rifles moved. About 5.30 a.m. the shelling became a heavy barrage, so that the Suffolks, who were lining the parapet ready to move in one long line, were ordered to take cover, and the O.C. 4th Suffolks tried to arrange for the advance to be made by platoons in succession from the left. This was being commenced when Zero occurred, and as the movement had not reached the 4th Suffolks he ordered the 2 front Companies to advance in platoons by rushes. The Right Companies began this, followed by a portion of the Supporting Companies, but the Left Company Commander was wounded, and, not having passed the order to any Officer, only a very small party of this Company went forward when the Right Company went. The small fragments that moved forward did well. They reached the line running North and South-West of LONE HOUSE, and the next line, BLACK WATCH CORNER - CARLISLE HOUSE, appearing unoccupied, they, after communicating with 4th King's Regt., moved into it, and did not have any casualties till they reached it, from snipers of a force to the Right Front, who looked at one time as if they would turn them out. The garrison of a strong post which had held up the 4th King's Regt. shortly afterwards surrendered to the 4th Suffolk party (11 and 2 Machine Guns), and they had taken 2 prisoners on reaching the trench.

At 12 noon the 2nd R.W.Fusiliers passed through this detachment, which then was withdrawing to rejoin Battalion Headquarters, but meeting an orderly with instructions to remain forward, they occupied a strong post near LONE HOUSE, and remained there till relieved next day by the 5th Scottish Rifles. Rations and water for 2 days were sent to them during night of 26/27th. There were two Officers with this party, Capt's Scrimgeour and Lake. The latter received a bullet wound in the wrist after taking the BLACK WATCH TRENCH.

The C.O. 4th Suffolks remained at and near 1st Middlesex Headquarters till about 10.45 a.m., when he rejoined his Headquarters at J.14 central, and began to reform the Battalion there as small parties came back. Some had not gone forward of the FITZCLARENCE Line; some had, and had remained in shell holes in front of it, having lost trace of their Companies and Officers in the mist and barrage, which was very heavy, chiefly from the East, but about 9.0 a.m. came from the South-East also. The main cause of some going further back was that O.C. Companies had not notified to their Companies the whereabouts of Battalion Headquarters, and men moved West by the road running South of GLENCORSE WOOD, along which line too wounded withdrew.

Officers (and later the C.O.) of the 11th West Yorks Regt. came about 3.0 p.m. to relieve the Battalion, and though one had an idea that a Company was to take over the trenches the Suffolks had occupied and improved on North and West of Battalion Headquarters, it appeared that they were to occupy the area on a different scheme, and in the end the Headquarters of the 8th Yorks Regt. took over Bn HQ

(3)

over Battalion Headquarters. The 4th Suffolks *about 9-0 p.m.* received orders to move out and withdraw to BEDFORD HOUSE Area, which was done at once, and in the end the Battalion reached BELLEGOED FARM - bivouac occupied on night 23/24th - by about 12.30 a.m. 29th instant.

30/9/17.   Lieut.Col.,
                              Commdg. 1/4th Suffolk Regiment.....

WAR DIARY
or
INTELLIGENCE SUMMARY.
(Erase heading not required.)

Place	Date	Hour	Summary of Events and Information	Remarks and references to Appendices
LYNDE	Oct 1st		Day spent in inspections and Platoon Training and a short Bn Parade.	
"	2nd		Parades in the morning. Baths in the afternoon at BLARINGHEM & clean clothes	
"	3rd		Bde inspected by the Commander in Chief at 11am. Sir Douglas Haig	
"	4th		Orders received to move to SETQUES, 6 miles S.W of ST OMER. These orders cancelled about midnight and others received to go to the forward area	
"	5th		Bn. entrained at EBBLINGHEM at 7.45am and detrained at YPRES at about 2/pm; then moved to dugouts in a railway embankment near Shrapnel Corner and came under orders of the 7th Division	
"	6th		Working parties commenced. These had to be found for the 525st Field Coy R.E. who were constructing a road through GLENCORSE WOOD Slabs of wood (1 per man per day) had to be carried from BIRR CROSS roads near HOOGE to the road head. Casualties for first day — 10 R. killed 7 OR wounded.	H. Greenaway Lt Col

Army Form C. 2118.

WAR DIARY
or
INTELLIGENCE SUMMARY.
(Erase heading not required.)

Place	Date	Hour	Summary of Events and Information	Remarks and references to Appendices
RAILWAY DUG OUTS	Oct 7		Very wet day. Working parties as usual.	
"	8		Working parties as usual. Evening parties postponed slightly owing to rain.	
"	9		Slightly better weather. Parties as usual. 1 O.R. Killed, 1 O.R. Wounded.	
"	10		Bad weather. Parties as usual.	
"	11		— — —	
"	12		At about 11:30 pm the 1st R.W.F arrived at the line stating that they had orders to come to the dugouts the Bn was in. They eventually settled in further down the embankment. Bad weather. Parties as usual. 1 O.R. Killed 1 O.R. Wounded. The minimum reserve under Capt H. Pretty left at 11am for KORTEPYP camp.	
"	13		Bad weather. Parties as usual.	
"	14		— — —	
"	15		Order received from C.R.E. 7th Division at 12.10 pm that the Bn would be relieved at about 12 noon that day. After numerous inquiries from the Division extd the 91st Bde who knew nothing about it	

J.R. Glennie Lt Col

WAR DIARY
or
INTELLIGENCE SUMMARY.
(Erase heading not required.)

Army Form C. 2118.

Place	Date	Hour	Summary of Events and Information	Remarks and references to Appendices
KORTEPYP CAMP	Oct 16th		The Bn was eventually relieved by the 7th Leicestershire Regt (S.N.T.) and moved in lorries to KORTEPYP Camp near NEUVE EGLISE arriving about 7pm.	
	17		Morning spent in Inspections. Shrapnels performed in afternoon at Y.M.C.A Hut.	
	18th		Parades in the morning. Bathing and clean clothes in the afternoon at the PALMER BATHS.	
			Parades as usual. Football match against 100th M.G.Coy in the afternoon. The Bn won 2-1. Capt H. Pretty left the Bn to take up the duties of 2nd in command of the 10th D.C.L.I. (Pioneers 3rd)	
	19th		Parades as usual. The C.O. and Coy commanders visited the left sector of the line in the morning. Capt F.S. Cubitt rejoined from 9th Inf Bde H/Q and assumed the duties of Second in command.	
	20		4 officers + 200 o.ranks on working parties constructing new Bn H.Q in the line, & making roads + null track under 11th + 212 th Coy R.E. Hours & remainder of Bn parades as usual.	

H. Chevasse Lt Col

Army Form C. 2118.

WAR DIARY
or
INTELLIGENCE SUMMARY.
(Erase heading not required.)

Instructions regarding War Diaries and Intelligence Summaries are contained in F. S. Regs., Part II. and the Staff Manual respectively. Title pages will be prepared in manuscript.

Place	Date	Hour	Summary of Events and Information	Remarks and references to Appendices
KORTEPYP CAMP. B	Oct 20th		The following Officers from 3rd NORFOLK REGT joined the Bn. 2nd LIEUTS. F J SMITH, O.C. MITCHELL, T.R. ABLETT, A.A. SHAW, C.H. ROBINSON, B. WEBB, F.S. WIGG, D.N. SEVERN.	PSC
	21st		Church Parade for 50 men per Coy in Church Army Hut. Battn. for transport H.Q. Coy "B" Coy. Weather fine & bright. The following awards were made by the Corps Commander. Bar to M.M. 202039 Pte PACKARD C. 201034 MARTIN C. 202069 Pte WHITING G.A. The MILITARY MEDAL 202222 SGT HERRING M, M.M. 2/Cpl DAVIES F. 200912 Pte WARD C.W. 201059 EVERETT W. 202324 Pte HALL A.E. 201389 ALEXANDER W. 201107 SICKAMORE G, 201967 ROUGHTON A.S. 202066 FRANCIS C.	PSC
	22nd		Inspections etc preparatory to going to trenches. Moved off by Platoons at 3:30 PM to relieve 1/9 H.L.I. in LEFT SECTOR. A. Coy on right, B/Coy in Centre, D Coy on left. C Coy support near Bn H.Q. Relief completed about 10:25 PM without any casualties. Weather fine.	PSC
	23rd		Rain in early morning June later. Trenches of right + centre Coys in fair order. Left badly battd + full of water. Bn H.Q. heavily shelled from 11:30 AM to 3:15 PM. Otherwise very quiet in Bn sector. a.8. again in evening.	PSC
	24th		Weather unsettled with some rain. Bn H.Q. again shelled from 2:15 AM to 3:0 PM. a few trench mortars + h/v shells along front line. Casualties, 1 rank killed. Owing to rain, water menaced in Left Coy trenches. Trench tracing + improvements in RIGHT + CENTRE Coys trenches continued. Casualties 1 o.r. killed.	PSC
	25th		Weather stormy. Bn sector quiet except for a few trench mortars near right Coy + Lt Cpl [illegible]	PSC

WAR DIARY
or
INTELLIGENCE SUMMARY.
(Erase heading not required.)

Army Form C. 2118.

Place	Date	Hour	Summary of Events and Information	Remarks and references to Appendices
	Oct 26th		Weather continues dull with much rain at times, causing trenches to collapse in many places. Relieved by 2nd A.S.H & went back to Bde Support but N. of MESSINES. Relief of front line completed 8.15 p.m. without too casualties	F.S.C.
	27th		Weather mild & cold. Bn. before trenches & draining in Bn area. Furnish working parties for R.E. & carrying parties to Bns in the line. Intermittent shelling but no casualties. A/Lt 609 Lilly & Lt deprest of 2 A.S.H. for tactical purposes. 2/Lieuts A. POTTER & S. YATES 3rd NORFOLK REGT. joined the Bn. Weather fine. Work continued as for 27th	P.P.6.
	28th			P.P.6. P.P.6.
	29th 30		Weather fine & cold. Work continued as for 20th. Weather fine till 11.0 am then much rain. Relieved by 2nd R.W.F. relief completed 8.45 p.m. No casualties. Bn moved to SHANKHILL HUTS, NEUVE EGLISE	P.P.6. P.P.6.
SHANKHILL HUTS NEUVE EGLISE.	31st		Boys employed cleaning up & inspections. Weather fine & bright	P.P.6.

In camp and billets
mSD. 14 September

Army Form C. 2118.

WAR DIARY
or
INTELLIGENCE SUMMARY.
(Erase heading not required.)

4 Dec R.I.R. Vol 26

Place	Date	Hour	Summary of Events and Information	Remarks and references to Appendices
SHANKHILL HUTS NEUVE EGLISE.	Nov 1st		Bn bathing & usual parade. Bandsmen for fife & drum band selected & commenced practice. Weather fine.	F.S.C.
	2nd		Bn moved by bus to MENIN GATE YPRES. Transport by road to BELGIAN CHATEAU. & came under orders of 1st ANZAC CORPS for work on roads. A Coy in new dug out & billets on E bank of moat + in tunnel under the WALL. B Coy in old houses in YPRES. C & D Coy in new dug out & billets under WALL. Bn H.Q. in new dug out & shelters on E bank of MOAT. H.Q. Coy in tunnel under WALL.	F.S.C.
			Bn H.Q. in new dug out shelters on E bank of MOAT. Intermittent shelling during night by H.V. gun. No casualties. Weather dull with slight rain most of the day. Band in pulling down huts of town – details for covers remained at NEUVE EGLISE.	F.S.C.
YPRES.	3rd		Bn found working parties of 4 officers + 550 o'ranks for road making + unloading lorries in the neighbourhood of WESTHOEK and CHATEAU WOOD. Casualties 2 o'ranks wounded. D Coy whose shelters were very poor + wet moved into old houses in YPRES. Weather dull + close.	F.S.C.
	4th		Working parties as for 3rd. Casualties 3 o'ranks wounded. Weather cold + misty in morning, bright + sunny in afternoon.	F.S.C.
"	5th		Working parties as usual. Casualties 2 L. YATES + 2 o'ranks wounded. L.G. Clare started for 2 men per coy. C. Coy have baths in YPRES in afternoon. Information received from 1st ANZAC CORPS that Bn will rejoin Division after work on 6th. Weather fine. No casualties.	F.S.C.
	6th		2 officers + 100 o'ranks employed on unloading lorries from limbers. Bn moved by bus to HILL 63 - NEUVE EGLISE. Transport by road to HILLSIDE CAMP NORTH, NEUVE EGLISE. Weather dull + rainy.	F.S.C.
NEUVE EGLISE.	7th 8th		Bns cleaning up & refitting. Coy parades in morning L.G. & Lewis lectures to coy Commanders + others in future work by Brigadier. Working parties of 75 + 50 o'ranks respectively. Weather dull with much rain in morning + night.	F.S.C.

WAR DIARY
or
INTELLIGENCE SUMMARY.
(Erase heading not required.)

Army Form C. 2118.

Place	Date	Hour	Summary of Events and Information	Remarks and references to Appendices
NEUVE EGLISE	Nov 9.		Coys parade as usual. Short route march. Working party as for 8th. Working party of 2 officers 70 o. ranks furnish at material on tram tramway for clothing. Football match of pd. Middx Rendt. Draw 2-2. Weather fine during day. rain at night.	FPG
	10		No training outside owing to heavy rain. Lectures & inspections in billets. Working party as for 8th.	PPG
	11		Shrill hands for so. ranks for long l. convact. Working party as for 2nd. Conference of all officers under C.O. on training & work in trenches. Neatley still with some rain.	PPG
MERRIS AREA	12		March to very scattered billets just west of METTEREN starting at about 9.15 am and arriving at about 1.30 pm. The Band played for the first time on the march. Weather very fine.	
	13		Ordinary parades during the morning. Small range used by snipers. Weather very fine.	
	14		C.O. and O.C. Coys visit the line to be taken over starting in a bus from Bde. HQ. at 8am. Parades as usual. Weather dull but fine.	
	15		Parades as usual. Range used by 2 Coys. Weather good. Lieut K.C. Shuttleworth joins Bn. for duty.	CW
POTIJZE	16.		Bn. Entrained on main road at 8am, proceeding in busses to just East of YPRES and marching to a camp at POTIJZE. Time of arrival about 3.30pm. Camp in bad condition (bivouacs)	

WAR DIARY
or
INTELLIGENCE SUMMARY.

Army Form C. 2118.

Place	Date	Hour	Summary of Events and Information	Remarks and references to Appendices
TRENCHES	17		Part of Transport moves back WEST of YPRES. Bn moves off at 2.45 pm and relieves 58th Canadians at ABRAHAM HEIGHTS (left support Bn.) Relief complete about 6.30 pm. Advanced party sent to front line about 8 pm and suffered the following casualties just outside left front Bn. Hq. (Hillside) 2/Lieut G.W. FISHER killed, 2/Lieut O.R. MITCHELL wounded. ~~4/Killed~~ 7 O.R's wounded. 10.12. 4 killed	Cdr.
	18.		Move off at about 4 pm and relieve 102 Canadians in left subsector. PASCHENDALE. Rations drawn and carried up from SEINE Dump by parties kept back from Coys for the purpose. Relief complete about 8 pm (a good relief.)	
	19.		Casualties:- Lieut K.C. SHUTTLEWORTH killed, 4 OR's killed, 3 OR's wounded.	
	20.		Casualties 9 OR's killed 23 OR's wounded	
	21.		Relieved by 2nd Arg: & Suth: High'rs and move back to ABRAHAM HEIGHTS. Relief complete about 7.30 pm. 2 Ot. Junior 19 O.R's wounded.	J.R. Chancemen M/C

WAR DIARY
or
INTELLIGENCE SUMMARY.
(Erase heading not required.)

Army Form C. 2118.

Place	Date	Hour	Summary of Events and Information	Remarks and references to Appendices
TRENCHES	22		C Coy moves up to CREST Fm and A Coy supplies a working party of 2 Platoons to help them dig fortifications and accomodation there after dusk. D Coy moves to vicinity of HAMBURGH, B Coy carrying up shelters for them to make accomodation with. 10 casualties	
POTIJZE	23		Relieved by 1st Cameronians. Relief complete about 7.30 p.m. Arrive in camp at POTIJZE about 9 p.m. Heavy shelling on the way out.	
TORONTO CAMP	24		Move off at 7.50am to ST JEAN and proceed from there by tram to BRANDHOEK. March to TORONTO Camp arriving about 10.30am.	
	25		Service at 10.15 am in YMCA Hut. Remainder of day spent in general cleaning up. Wet and windy day.	
	26		Usual parades during the morning as much in huts as possible owing to bad weather.	
	27		Parades during the morning.	

J.N. Greenaway H/Col

Army Form C. 2118.

WAR DIARY
or
INTELLIGENCE SUMMARY.
(Erase heading not required.)

Instructions regarding War Diaries and Intelligence Summaries are contained in F. S. Regs., Part II. and the Staff Manual respectively. Title pages will be prepared in manuscript.

Place	Date	Hour	Summary of Events and Information	Remarks and references to Appendices
TORONTO CAMP	28		Baths and clean clothes for all. Parades during the morning.	C4
"	29		Parades during the morning.	
POTIJZE	30.		Move at 8.15 am by road to a camp at POTIJZE arriving at about 11am. near St JEAN.	

In Command 14GC
1/4 Suffolk Regt.
30/4/17.

WAR DIARY or INTELLIGENCE SUMMARY

Army Form C. 2118.

4 Suffolk Regt
Vol 27

Place	Date 1917	Hour	Summary of Events and Information	Remarks and references to Appendices
POTIZJE St JEAN CAMP	Dec 1		All available men on working parties. Casualties nil. Weather cold.	FPC
	2		No church service. Church parade. At 5:30 pm ordered to be ready to move up into line at ½ hours notice. This cancelled 5:30 pm. Very cold with strong wind.	FPC
	3		Working parties as before. Casualties nil. Sharp hard ground.	FPC
	4		Improvements carried out in camp drainage. Bell tents brought for troops hitherto in bivouacs. Inoculations for "Trench fever" — Men of Coy B &C now in vogue.	FPC
	5		Reconnaissance of neighbourhood of SEINE C.T.B. 10-10 P.D for subsequent tracks in midground. Much new front line troops on edge of marshy ground which was not covered by front line troops. Transport Lines moved to POTIZJE on YPRES - ZONNEBEKE Rd. Head quart. Casualties nil.	FPC
	6		Relieved 2 QUEENS in front line. A+D in front. C in support. B reserve. 10 had wounded. Thawing very muddy.	FPC
In the line PASSCHENDAELE	7		Moved tied to support near SEINE Bn H.Q at HAMBURG. 10 O.R. wounded. Ramy.	FPC
	8		Moved up to front line in PASSCHENDAELE Ruinoir 2 Coys, 1st Btn and 2 Coys, 16 KRRC. B.C.D in front line A in support. 2.O.Rs wounded. Fine but very muddy.	FPC
	9		Moved tied to support at HAMBURG. Gnrts. wounded. Weather fine.	FPC
	10		Remained in support. Thus line during this time considerably quieter than in previous tour. Weather fine but dull.	FPC
	11		Moved back to camp at POTIZJE. Relieved by 5 Bt. Durham LI. No casualties during relief. Weather fine but dull+cold.	FPC

J.R. Openson LtCol

Army Form C. 2118.

WAR DIARY
or
INTELLIGENCE SUMMARY.
(Erase heading not required.)

Instructions regarding War Diaries and Intelligence Summaries are contained in F. S. Regs., Part II. and the Staff Manual respectively. Title pages will be prepared in manuscript.

Place	Date '17	Hour	Summary of Events and Information	Remarks and references to Appendices
POTIJZE	Dec 12		Bn entrained at St JEAN at 10-30 PM & detrained at GODEWAERSVELDE, thence marching to very scattered billets between STEENVOORDE - EECKE - St SYLVESTRE CAPPEL. Bold & dull.	FFG FFC
EECKE	13		Companies cleaning up. Weather dull & cold.	FFC
	14		Coys training in morning. Platoon football competitions started in afternoon. Night firing in morning. Wet but dull in afternoon.	FFG
	15		Training as usual. Fine & bright, very cold.	FFC
	16		Church Parade in morning. 7 Coy moved to billets & Sec nearer billets vacated by gunners who were in our area. Major Cullet assumed command during his absence. Training as usual. Night snow during night. Bull held.	FFG
	17		6 NCOs proceeded on leave. Major Cullet assumed command during his absence. Training as usual. Night snow during night.	FFG
	18		B & C Coys went musketry & D Company Parades. Had pst. A & B Chd D on Lewis gun musketry practice with L.C.O. for tactical scheme. All officers except one few Coys parading under Bde. P.T. & F Instructor. Remainder of Companies bombing & rifle grenade instruction. Frost continues.	FFB
	19			FFB.
	20		A & D went marching. B & C Company knowing Lecture by Major Ser. Pinkham on CAMBRAI fighting in afternoon at EECKE. Lewis pst. B.C. moved to billets.	FFB
	21		B & D on range at BOIS DE BEAUVOORDE. A & C Company Parades & rifle inspection by Armourer Sergt. Lecture to officers & NCO's in evening by Bde Gas Officer. Hard frost.	FGC
	22		A & C route marching. B & D Company training, warning, infection: Frost.	FFG
	23		Bde Ceremonial Parade at EECKE. Divisional Commander General, mislaid ribbons to Capt Harrison 13 Coy mbs. Afterwards Bde marched past Major General Pinney MC in EECKE. Very cold, & party.	FFB

Jo. Commoner Lt Colonel

WAR DIARY
or
INTELLIGENCE SUMMARY.

(Erase heading not required.)

Army Form C. 2118.

Instructions regarding War Diaries and Intelligence Summaries are contained in F.S. Regs., Part II. and the Staff Manual respectively. Title pages will be prepared in manuscript.

Place	Date	Hour	Summary of Events and Information	Remarks and references to Appendices
EECKE	Dec 24		Bde Routs marched in morning. Duel Read Played Bn HQ in afternoon. A & C v Bde Football competition. W.O. v. Cold. Thawing.	APC
	25		Voluntary Church Service in morning. Major Jen Penny billeted to give Xmas greetings. Company Xmas Dinners in afternoon. A Coy beats 1/f 2 A&SH running horz in Bde Football competition 3-1. Thaw continues, but more snow showers from 3.0 pm onwards.	APC
	26		Owing to show W.O. Training parade curtailed. Bde Road were flooded. Bn had entered a team cancelled on account of snow. Letters to Officers.	APC
	27		NCO in evening. "Tommy Cookers" supplied by Bde by Officers Mess now during day. All officers except one for the Coys attended Lecture + demonstration of XVII Corps School. Boys have gun. Whole BdHQ at Bde for hot bath. Not so cold. Re-armed more than during the day.	APC
	28		A + C Coys & L Gunners on range. B + D to Thawing more from road B + D Coys on range A + C. Played training W.O. Training 1	APC APC
	29		Rifle + W.M.S.	APC
	30		Church Parade for 30 men in bay at EECKE. Thawing but very cold.	APC
	31		Company Parade Major Potts returned specialist movement. Freezing hard NE wind very cold.	APC

WAR DIARY
or
INTELLIGENCE SUMMARY.

1/4th SUFFOLK REGT.

Army Form C. 2118.

Place	Date	Hour	Summary of Events and Information	Remarks and references to Appendices
EECKE	JAN. 1ST 1918		Being New Year's day there were no parades. In the afternoon the baths were allotted to the battalion. Weather continued cold & frosty. Lieuts. W. WASP & S.G. WASS L & R. joined the battalion	F.P
EECKE	JAN. 2ND		Weather cold. Companies trained as far as weather permitted. Lt-Col H.C. COPEMAN. D.S.O returned from leave. In New Years Honours list Lt-Col H.C. COPEMAN D.S.O was appointed Companion to the Most Distinguished Order of Saint Michael & Saint George for services rendered in connection with military operations in the field. Dated Jan 1st 1918	F.P
EECKE	JAN 3RD		All officers (except one per company) & selection of O.R. attended a demonstration of an aeroplane flying at various heights, with a view to assisting infantry in engaging hostile aircraft from the ground. Weather very cold & more snow fell.	F.P
EECKE	JAN. 4TH		Company parades in morning. Lewis gunners on range.	F.P

A. Copeman Lt.

Army Form C. 2118.

WAR DIARY
or
INTELLIGENCE SUMMARY.
(Erase heading not required.)

1/4TH SUFFOLK REGT

Instructions regarding War Diaries and Intelligence Summaries are contained in F.S. Regs., Part II. and the Staff Manual respectively. Title pages will be prepared in manuscript.

Place	Date	Hour	Summary of Events and Information	Remarks and references to Appendices
EECKE	JAN 5TH		Entrained & started at 12.45 P.M for BRANDHOEK AREA getting into TORONTO CAMP. W. at 3.10 P.M. Bitterly cold night. Capt H. PRETTY + Capt L.J. RICHARDS were awarded the military cross in New Years Honours list	F.P.
TORONTO CAMP	JAN 6TH		Church parade in Y.M.C.A. hut at 9.45 A.M. Very cold morning + hard frost, in the afternoon it commenced to rain.	F.P.
TORONTO CAMP	JAN 7TH		Physical training & lectures were all that the condition of the ground allowed. In the evening it commenced to freeze again & the night was very cold. The following names appeared in the New Years Honour's List as mentioned in Despatches. Lieut-Colonel H.C. COPEMAN. C.M.G. D.S.O, 200538 L/Sergt W.F. BUTCHER, 200055 Sergt C.K. ROE, 2nd Lieut N.G. ARMSTONG joined the battalion	F.P.
TORONTO CAMP	JAN 8TH		Snowing & cold. Companies did Physical Training, Musketry & lectures in the huts	F.P.
TORONTO CAMP	JAN 9TH		Companies at disposal of company commanders. Snowed all afternoon	F.P.

Army Form C. 2118.

WAR DIARY
or
INTELLIGENCE SUMMARY.
(Erase heading not required.)

1/4th SUFFOLK R^{gt}

Place	Date	Hour	Summary of Events and Information	Remarks and references to Appendices
TORONTO CAMP	JAN 10TH		Entrained & proceeded to forward area; accommodated in huts & tents at WHITBY CAMP a little N.E. of YPRES. Arrived in camp 11 A.M. relieving the 20TH R.F.'s.	T.P.
WHITBY CAMP	JAN 11TH		Furnished working parties numbering 130 O.R. Remainder worked on improvement of camp. Weather dull.	T.P.
WHITBY CAMP	JAN 12TH		Morning spent in preparation of fur at the order trench for that. Moved by companies starting at 4.25 P.M. & relieved the 16TH K.R.R.C. in support at HAMBURG. Relief complete 8.35 P.M.	T.P.
HAMBURG SUPPORT LINE	JAN 13TH		Moved at 5.45 P.M. & relieved the 1ST Queen's in right sector of front line. Relief complete at 8.35 P.M. B, A & C Coy in front line, D Coy in support. Weather very cold & some snow. 1 O.R. wounded.	T.P.
TRENCHES	JAN 14TH		Snowed in morning, with a thaw & rain mid-day. 1 O.R. wounded.	T.P.

WAR DIARY
INTELLIGENCE SUMMARY.
(Erase heading not required.)

1/4th SUFFOLK RET.

Army Form C. 2118.

Place	Date	Hour	Summary of Events and Information	Remarks and references to Appendices
TRENCHES	JAN 15TH		Rained in morning, increasing towards evening to a downpour accompanied by a gale of wind. Constant work had to be done on posts & trenches to keep them all habitable. 1 O.R. wounded	4P
TRENCHES	JAN 16TH		Weather dull & some rain in morning. 1 O.R. killed	4P
TRENCHES	JAN 17TH		Relieved by the 5th Scottish Rifles. Relief commenced at 6 P.M & was complete by 9.5 P.M. We then proceeded to LOW FARM where we entrained for ALNWICK CAMP, N.E of YPRES arriving 11.20 P.M & were accommodated in Miners huts & tents. Camp very wet & muddy. During the day there was much snow & rain.	4P
ALNWICK CAMP	JAN 18TH		Day spent fact-making, generally cleaning up as far as conditions allowed	4P

WAR DIARY
or
INTELLIGENCE SUMMARY. 1/4TH SUFFOLK REGT
(Erase heading not required.)

Army Form C. 2118.

Place	Date	Hour	Summary of Events and Information	Remarks and references to Appendices
ALNWICK CAMP	JAN 19TH		Entrained at 10 A.M & moved to Toronto Camp. W. Brandhoek area. All in about 12 min day. B.C & D. Coys got baths & clean clothing. Weather still dull but no rain.	7.P.
TORONTO CAMP	JAN 20TH		Church service in Y.M.C.A hut at 10 A.M. "A" Coy baths. The following were awarded the Military Medal under date 3.12.17. 200313 Pte HART.A. 200256 Pte FRYATT.S. 200551 Sgt CRACKNELL.A.T. 200299 L/Cpl LEGGETT.W.J. 202067 Pte HART U.P. H.H. 201099 Sgt KERRIDGE.G. and under date 22.12.17. 201405 Sgt LAST. W. Officers, Warrant officers, N.C.O's & men subscribed & sent a donation of £70-15-0 to the funds of the Red Cross societies. 6 O.R. joined the bn for duty.	7.P.
TORONTO CAMP	JAN 21ST		Entrained & proceeded ALNWICK CAMP front train left BRANDHOEK AREA 2 P.M & regiment was all in by 3.45 P.M	7.P.

N. Green Capt/Lt

Army Form C. 2118.

WAR DIARY
INTELLIGENCE SUMMARY.
1/4TH SUFFOLK REGT

(Erase heading not required)

Instructions regarding War Diaries and Intelligence Summaries are contained in F. S. Regs., Part II. and the Staff Manual respectively. Title pages will be prepared in manuscript.

Place	Date	Hour	Summary of Events and Information	Remarks and references to Appendices
ALNWICK CAMP	JAN 22ND		Working parties numbering 145 O.R were furnished for work in forward area. Remainder at work improving camp.	T.P.
ALNWICK CAMP	JAN 23RD		Foot rubbing preparatory to going forward occupied the morning. (IRKSOME #2) Bn moved at 4 P.M & relieved 9TH H.L.I in support at HAMBURG Relief completed 6.40. Defence Scheme for support bn in this sector, two coys ready to counter-attack & 2 coys for carrying for front line battalions.	T.P.
HAMBURG SUPPORT	JAN 24TH		Weather fine & line quiet.	HAMBURG T.P.
HAMBURG SUPPORT	JAN 25TH		Weather fine & line quiet	T.P.

J.R. [signature]

Army Form C. 2118.

WAR DIARY
or
INTELLIGENCE SUMMARY.
(Erase heading not required.)

1/4th SUFFOLK REGT

Instructions regarding War Diaries and Intelligence Summaries are contained in F. S. Regs., Part II. and the Staff Manual respectively. Title pages will be prepared in manuscript.

Place	Date	Hour	Summary of Events and Information	Remarks and references to Appendices
HAMBURG SUPPORT	JAN. 26TH		Weather rather foggy. Line quiet.	F.P.
HAMBURG SUPPORT	JAN 27TH		Weather remained misty. Line quiet.	F.P.
HAMBURG SUPPORT	JAN 28TH		Relieved by 5th Northumberland Fusiliers. Relief complete at 7.45. Battalion then marched to Low Farm & entrained on light railway & proceeded to ST LAWRENCE CAMP. BRANDHOEK AREA getting into camp 11.35 P.M. Casualty. 1 O.R. wounded by machine gun bullet leaving HAMBURG. First line transport entrained at VLAMERTINGHE & left for back area at 4.45 P.M.	F.P.
ST LAWRENCE CAMP	JAN 29TH		Day spent cleaning up. Second line transport left by road for back area starting at 7.15 A.M. Fine sunny day.	F.P.
ST LAWRENCE CAMP	JAN 30TH		Moved at 4.5. P.M & marched to BRANDHOEK where the regiment entrained & left at 6.25 P.M. proceeding to WIZERNES arriving 10.55.P.M. Detrained 12.45 A.M. The R. Gran---an H.B.L.	F.P.

Army Form C. 2118.

WAR DIARY
or
INTELLIGENCE SUMMARY.   1/4th SUFFOLK REGT

(Erase heading not required.)

Instructions regarding War Diaries and Intelligence Summaries are contained in F. S. Regs., Part II. and the Staff Manual respectively. Title pages will be prepared in manuscript.

Place	Date	Hour	Summary of Events and Information	Remarks and references to Appendices
	JAN 30th (continued)		buses which were expected to convey the regiment to its destination were not available & after waiting till 4 a.m. it was decided to march. At 5 a.m. some buses overtook us on the road & three companies finished the journey in them, the remaining company marching. The final destination NOIR CARME – ZUDAUSQUES & other hamlets was reached & everybody in billets by 7.15 a.m. after a very tiring journey. The night was very cold but otherwise fine.	79.
NOIRE CARME	JAN 31st		Day spent resting & cleaning up. Beautiful weather.	N.T.R.

for Commanding [signature]
Col. 1/4 Suffolk Regt

www.ingramcontent.com/pod-product-compliance
Lightning Source LLC
Chambersburg PA
CBHW081525160426
43191CB00011B/1686